THEOSOPHY
AND WORLD-PROBLEMS

*Being the four Convention Lectures delivered in
Benares at the Forty-Sixth Anniversary of
the Theosophical Society, December, 1921*

BY

ANNIE BESANT

C. JINARĀJADĀSA

J. KRISHNAMURTI

G. S. ARUNDALE

Fredonia Books
Amsterdam. The Netherlands

Theosophy and World-Problems

by
Annie Besant
C. Jinarajadasa
J. Krishnamurti
G. S. Arundale

ISBN: 1-58963-338-5

Copyright © 2001 by Fredonia Books

Reprinted from the 1922 edition

Fredonia Books
Amsterdam, The Netherlands
http://www.fredoniabooks.com

THEOSOPHY AND WORLD-PROBLEMS

CONTENTS

———

CONTENTS

THEOSOPHY AND WORLD-PROBLEMS

FRIENDS :

I have taken as the title of my lecture, Theosophy and World-Problems, and you will at once realise that I think that a solution is possible, and that, as President of the Theosophical Society, I am likely to see that solution in the teachings of the Divine Wisdom, or Theosophy. When I say "World-Problems," I mean problems that you find practically in all civilised Nations, all Nations that have reached a certain level of thought, emotion and conduct. In every one of these there are certain questions which are occupying the minds of the thoughtful, of the philosophical, of the religious, and they are practically the same in all the Nations. They do not deal with details, but with principles. They are founded on certain general ideas of the relationship between man and man, not for the moment between Nation and Nation. You have of course in addition to these the great problems of Internationalism, in which every Nation has an interest—its relation to other Nations; and there you have a subject of great complexity, but one which has its ideal to study and to understand. Now these

World-Problems are those which affect, in the path that I am taking, the relation between man and man, between class and class, between sect and sect, within the boundaries of a Nation. That is the part of our subject with which I have chosen to deal, and in dealing with a single Nation on these questions, I am really dealing with all. But in so dealing, we are confronted with the ruins of a civilisation based on certain definite ideals, worked by certain definite methods, that are lying behind us, and we can study the results of these principles and methods in the state of the world at the present time. We have to deal with the fact that the civilisation, which largely crashed down in the Great War, is crumbling to pieces under the present unrest. Some time ago it might have been perceived to have reached a stage in each department of life, from which it could go no further along its particular line. You may remember that, some years ago now, I gave a series of lectures in London, and I called them "The Changing World," and in that I dealt with civilisation as it was, the civilisation which may specifically be called that of the individual. In the various great departments of human life, I tried to show that we had gone as far as we could go along those particular lines, and had reached what I called a deadlock in each, a stage in which we had, so to speak, to recreate our ideals and our methods; to find a new basis for civilisation; to discover new methods by which it should be carried on : new methods which would appeal to the great masses of mankind. What I shall say to-day in a single lecture will be a suggestion of those new ideals, those new methods and those new motives, of the changed basis from which we must start, of the changed ideals towards which our progress must be directed, of the changed methods which we are to apply to human nature, so that it may respond to our appeals and go along a new path of civilisation. Of course, in a single lecture, one can only sketch a thing very roughly; but those who come after me will deal with some special problems, some special aspects of the new civilisation, while I am rather trying to take a general look over the field, and see what are the main problems that have to be solved, problems without a solution of which mankind can only go down into ruin, and be faced with hopeless despair. Looking at these, we may sum them up under a few heads, which cover a very, very large space.

We have to deal with the problem of Authority, of Obedience to Authority, of what we may call the general problem of Leadership. What is a leader ? Whence is his authority to be drawn ? Whence is his power to be derived ? For where you have collective action in Nations, you must have some one who corresponds to a leader of some kind, and he must have something in him which gives him a right to take the lead.

Then we have all those problems which deal with the production and distribution of wealth : economic problems—Production, which comes under Industry, Distribution, which comes under Commerce. On these the physical well-being of the Nation depends as long as we live in physical bodies ; these cannot possibly be ignored. Then we have to consider all the questions of Education, which I am not going to deal with, for I leave them to Mr. Arundale, who is more qualified to deal with them than I am. Then we come to the question of Law and Conscience, which in every great time of transition is raised—innumerable questions which have to be solved well for the future civilisation. I am in search of a principle which can be laid down, by which conflict between law and conscience may be avoided, if it be possible to avoid it, or at least its dangers to some extent neutralised, by pointing out the function of law and the function of conscience in human life. And that brings us very close to the whole great problem of the relation between the Individual and the State. How far is the authority of the State to go ? What do you mean by State, when you say State ? Do you mean Government or Nation ? Because the answer must very, very largely depend on your definition of the word State, and it is defined in different ways by different students of political science, and that naturally makes us glance for a moment at the question of civil organisation. How is *that* to be put on a firm basis ? And amid all the changing opinions in the controversies of the day, how are we to decide our own path? What are we to advocate to our fellow-men? How are we to serve our day and our generation, we, who claim to have a fuller knowledge from our study, a deeper insight, than the ordinary statesman and politician of the time? You see we are here dealing with problems of enormous importance, of immense complexity; not for India only, at the present time, but for all the Nations of the world they are of vital importance. For here we are dealing not with words, but with the very facts of life. It is not difficult to deceive an ignorant crowd with phrases, but you cannot juggle with natural laws by phrases. The laws of Nature work themselves out, and pay very small attention to the statements of politicians, of statesmen, of theorists; and while it is very easy to mislead and delude an ignorant crowd with words which are not definitely related to facts, it is not so easy to convince them of the results that grow out of the blunders, the errors and the follies which such a crowd may carry out under the impulse of words, which have not facts and reality behind them. This means anarchy, misery all round; this means throwing the Nation back, delaying perhaps for a century its advance, even if it does not go down, as so many Nations of the past have gone down, into absolute death of Nationality and disappearance from the map of mankind.

Now some people would say : What have all these questions to do with Theosophy ? Everything ! Most people who have studied deeply, most Hindūs, at least, who have studied their traditions and history, believe that the world is ruled by a great body of divinely illuminated Men; they speak of the Ṛṣhis, whom they read about in their ancient books; they find that these Rshis are not people who wander about in the clouds having no relation to ordinary human life, but that on the contrary They have been particularly active in human life, and that They have particular functions, special to each, in the various departments of the life of man and of Nations. Theosophy, which is derived from the Wisdom of these Ṛṣhis, cannot therefore be unconcerned with any department of human life. It embraces everything; and if that great Hierarchy is concerned in the fate of Nations, in the progress of events, in the shaping of civilisations, in the guidance of evolution, then those who are its servants have also to labour in all these many departments of human life. Following that wise phrase of an ancient Hebrew Scripture, which speaks of the Wisdom as the " wisdom that mightily and sweetly ordereth all things," we see that it is the duty of the Theosophists of the present time, each man in his own particular depart-ment, with his intellectual and moral equipment, to play his part in the fate of his own country primarily, and of all other countries generally; and thus to help the world through the present dangerous state of transition, crossing that tumultuous sea of unrest on the bark of Principles that is able to outride the storm. If we cannot do that, I fail to see of what use our studies for all these many years have been. We are now at our Forty-sixth Anniversary, and if we have not learnt something of the Wisdom, of the Wisdom that we profess to teach, then I am afraid we are very unprofitable servants, that have not fulfilled the object with which we were given the opportunity of studying this Divine Wisdom.

Look with me for a moment at the present condition of Society, which has been for some time past coming to certain definite ends, has, as it were, among those who have been blindly following, taken people to different goals. In thinking generally of what we may call the civilisation of the fifth branch of the fifth Root Race in the West, we shall find that specially it is marked out, among the civilisations of the world, as individualistic and competitive. I am not at all going to quarrel with that; ugly as it is in many respects, quarrelsome as it is in many respects, it is a necessary stage in the evolution of mankind. For what have we learnt from our studies of Theosophy as regards that number "five" that I have just mentioned? We have learnt to connect with it in the human constitution the concrete or scientific mind in man, that which the Hindū calls the lower Manas—the lower mind; and it is that lower mind which in the fifth sub-race—the Teutonic, has reached a point beyond any that it had reached in average humankind in earlier races. During our own life-time—the elder amongst us—enormous advances have been made in science. Discoveries have been piled upon discoveries. New methods, new powers have been found and brought under the control of man. But in all that discovery and all that gaining of control, the object of it has not been the benefit of mankind, so much as the advancement of knowledge, which might be applied to the good, or prosperity, I should say, of the particular Nation in which the researches were carried on. Now on that point I must guard myself to some extent. There are great men of science, men like Wallace, Crookes, Darwin, Huxley, Bose, and some others, whose aim has been the increase of knowledge in order that mankind as a whole may be benefited by it. We must not ignore that in any criticism that we are making; nothing is more admirable than their patience. Nothing finer than their insight. Their intellect is something marvellous, their accomplishments are wonderful. But a good many years ago, when Mr. A. P. Sinnett, our late Vice-President, asked his Master whether He would not help the scientific men of his time, whether He would not give some indications of lines which might be pursued, which would prove valuable in the way of discovery, the answer he received was remarkable. I cannot quote the exact words, but the sense of the answer was : " We will never help ordinary science, until the human conscience is more highly developed." Those who have watched the late war will realise how wise was that refusal, for all the scientific men of Europe strove with each other chiefly to make new discoveries, each for his own Nation, discoveries in explosive compounds, in poisonous gases, in every method of destruction, in order to slaughter a larger number of their fellow-men. All the resources of science were turned to that end, not to assist but to kill, not to save but to slaughter, not to remedy but to destroy ; and no thought of ruth for human pain, no thought of mercy or of compassion hindered that frightful research into the hidden power of a natural object to tear down and not to build. The scientific world is on the verge of discovery—although everything possible will be done to prevent the discovery being made—of how to break up the atom, how to liberate the forces which hold the atom together. If they succeed, they will be able to liberate forces by which a single person can loose energy which will lay the whole of a huge city in ruins and kill every human being in it. A delightful discovery for a lover of mankind to make ! They are looking for an admirable compound, which can be taken up in an aeroplane, so that bombs containing it may explode in the air, and spread heavy poisonous gases over a great area, so that a whole regiment of an army may be murdered by the explosion of *one* of those fiendish bombs. If that is the best that civilisation and science can do, I should be inclined to agree with Mr. Gandhi that the sooner they come to an end the better. We see how wise were the Master's words. Let the moral conscience develop before knowledge goes further. For naturally when the moral conscience is developed, science will become the handmaid of human happiness, as it ought to be in a Nation of morality and of character.

Looking at it in that way, we may realise why this particular type of civilisation is breaking down, without possibility of revival. We have come to a point where we cannot afford to go any further along that particular road, for it leads to mutual destruction among the leading Nations of mankind. War must cease. Arbitration must be substituted for War, Justice for Force.

Looking from quite another standpoint, we see that the outcome of Production by many for individualistic profit is, in every Nation, the rise, by private ownership of the means of production, of a class far too wealthy, with the inevitable other side of the shield, the great masses seething in poverty intolerable, which ought to be made impossible. These are the results looked at coldly, at the end, so to speak, of this civilisation. Why then did I say it was a necessary stage? Because it was necessary for further progress that the human concrete mind should be developed; because by its very nature it develops by struggle and in combat; because in the older civilisations the ideas of duty, obligation, submission, had gone too far and had led to tyranny on one side and servility upon the other, and it was necessary that this should be corrected. The next stage of human evolution was that of the concrete mind, the lower Manas, which must develop its power, and on that foundation an individualistic civilisation must needs be built. So we had a religion founded upon the same fundamental truths as the former religions, but emphasising the *value* of the individual rather than his *obligations*. The value of the individual soul is put in the very forefront of the teaching: "What shall it profit a man, if he gain the whole world and lose his own soul, or what shall a man give in exchange for his soul?" That is why, as I have often before remarked, the doctrine of reincarnation became submerged in Christianity; while you find it in various forms in the teachings of the early writers of the Church, it was branded as a heresy by a Church Council in the sixth century, and was forgotten by the orthodox Christians. You can see how necessary that was for the growth of this strong combative individuality. For if you have a large number of lives, each individual life loses something of its importance, since what you fail to do in one life, you may accomplish in another. If you have only one life, and if on that life your everlasting destiny depends, the destiny of everlasting happiness or everlasting misery, then this one short human life becomes of supreme importance, and although the reason cannot ultimately admit the justice of such a scheme, still it would enormously stimulate effort, and the main result would be a great increase in the sense of the value of the single individual life, and thus would come about the development of great individual strength.   And thus evolution of the lower mind went on all through the Middle Ages in Europe.   These are the centuries called "the Dark Ages," but it must be remembered that while there was little science, except among the Muhammadans, philosophy and metaphysics reached a very high point, both among the Christian scholars and thinkers, the Islāmic metaphysicians, and some Hebrews of genius.   Though there were intellectual giants in those days, the masses of the people were deplorably ignorant, and of the priesthood it was said that in the days of Alfred of England, there was scarcely a priest south of the Thames who understood the Latin tongue—the sacred language of his Faith.   With the revival of concrete knowledge came gradually the rise of what is called Democracy, which only organised itself from the end of the eighteenth century, and with growing power insisted on having education, and thus the general level of mind was raised.

Looking closely into the underlying principles of European civilisation, we find that the very basic idea underlying it, moulded as it was by the Christianity, not so much of the Christ as of His Church as it formulated its doctrines into a logical whole, was that man was fundamentally evil. This is the basic idea, and it colours all methods. You may read it still in the Articles of the English Church, which on this matter is not yet reformed, that in every child of Adam—because out of him, the common father of humanity, we are supposed to descend—there is a certain "fault and corruption of nature," whereby man is very far gone from original righteousness, and is of his own nature inclined to evil. The infant inherits this natural sinfulness, and it is very frankly put that "in every person born into this world, it deserveth God's wrath and damnation". Thus the whole human race is under the wrath of God. I do not mean that most Christians now believe this to be true, but that it remains in the doctrine of the Church and ignorant people do really believe it. On that fundamental error all the subsidiary errors of this view of man are based. Law is wanted to restrain men from behaving like wild beasts, for there is a natural tendency in men to live upon others like beasts of prey, quarrelling with each other, fighting with each other. Even Tennyson spoke of letting the ape and tiger in us die. That is the aim of the good man, and the fundamental idea that man is evil poisons the whole system. It is true that there is such an element in us, but it is superficial, not essential. It is not man's *nature* to be wicked and full of hatred, preying on his fellows. Man is essentially Divine. Looking on man as naturally evil poisons the very roots of action, founding it on a falsehood, and leading to base motives. The sinfulness of our progenitor comes down like a hereditary disease to every father and mother; they hand it on to their children, whom they brought into the world. One result was the using as motive the appeal to the selfishness in man, and not the appeal to the self-sacrifice. How often have we seen it declared that " you must move a crowd by appealing to the selfishness in human nature. You must show them what they *get* by the action you want them to adopt. You must show them what advantage will accrue to them. You cannot move the mass of people by unselfish motives." And that is natural, if man be corrupt at his heart, as one of the great Scripture writers has said, that man's heart is " deceitful above all things and desperately wicked ". What can anyone do with a race, evil in its inmost nature, except by appealing to motives belonging to the lower nature, and thus inducing it to move in the right direction by threats and bribes ? The profit and the prizes that might be won by strength and gained by subtlety, by trampling over the weak and the more helpless, were motives that were all justified as " natural," as inevitable in human society, and the qualities evolved by ruthless competition are pointed to as the justification of the present economic system, though they hinder the unfolding of the Divine in man. Yet every public speaker knows that a crowd rises to an appeal to heroism and sacrifice, that miners spring forward to risk their lives to save a comrade, just because the appeal is to the "Hidden God," and He responds.

Now all that is a necessary stage. The mind had to be evolved, because the next great stage in human evolution, the appearance of Buḍḍhi, the unifying force, could not be reached until the strong individual was evolved. Nature, it is often said, makes no leaps. She must go from rung to rung up the great ladder of evolution. So we have this combative civilisation, this struggling of one against the other, the weakest continually going down as the wheel turns, until they are seething in a poverty more terrible than the world has ever known before, amid wealth so great in the hands of the few, that they cannot find ways of using it. That is the civilisation that is passing, having done its work; and now we have either to go forward or backward. We cannot continue as we are. It is too intolerable to be borne. Some people want to go backward. They say all this modern civilisation is really a curse.

So they say : " Let us go back to the simple life. Let us wear as little cloth as possible, and feed on as simple food as possible. Let us live like villagers, like peasants, let us get rid of all the things that this concrete mind has been discovering for these hundreds of years." This is what I may call the physical side of Mr. Gandhi's ideals. You can read it in that interesting book of his called *Indian Home Rule*. He wants to get rid of all machinery, to go back to the simple action of a spinning-wheel and hand-loom. He wants to confine people to hand-made goods and to have no machine-goods at all, because he regards machinery as devilish. He wants to have no government, because all government is satanic. He does not want any modern science, nor any doctors, for hospitals are also the work of the devil, and the drugs given by doctors are more mischievous than useful. If a man is dying let him die, says he, because it only means that there is one person less in the world, and there are a great many of them. He wishes that we all should go back to the ordinary pastoral stage of a long-ago civilisation, the simple village life which was a stage in the growth of mankind. Everything else is to be swept away; and even artificial means of locomotion are undesirable, because God has given you two legs, and it is your business to walk on them. I know it sounds absurd, when you put it sentence after sentence in this way, but it is moving great masses of people who do not in the least understand what it means, but who know that they are suffering, and have a blind faith in his imagined " supernatural powers " of which he has given no sign. But the question for us is what is the ideal towards which we should move, and his ideal is the going back to a very simple state of human life. We cannot stand still. We must either go backward or forward. Well, many of us do not wish to go back. We do not wish to force the cultured to the level of the illiterate, but to raise the illiterate to the many-aspected life of the cultured. We do not wish to make the rich poor, but to lift the poor so that they may share the comforts and refinements of the life of the highest class ; we do not wish to go back into a simpler, more animal, and merely primitive condition, with a few mighty and outstanding geniuses, but to develop all to a level of high intellectual and emotional life.

Now what must going forward mean ? It must mean starting from an entirely different basis as regards the conception of man. It means the lifting up of a new Ideal, the declaration that man is fundamentally divine and not devilish. That in the heart of man God is living, and that the true life of man is to be the manifestation of that divine Spirit, embodied in the vehicles that he uses. That that divine life in him is ever striving upwards, and that the duty of the teacher, of the speaker, of the orator, is to appeal to the highest motives in man and not to the lowest, to awaken a response from the living God in him, who is sometimes described as a sleeping God

B

in man's heart. Then, even as it were in his sleep, he will hear the dream-call which awakens, the bugle-cry of sacrifice, and for love's sake he will answer to that with joy, for sacrifice is the life of the Spirit, on which the whole world depends. Thus our very base of Society is changed. We no longer look on our fellow-men as fundamentally evil, but as fundamentally divine. We no longer base our appeal on selfish motives, but on unselfish. We no longer put, as the aim of a man, work for his own ends no matter what happens to all round him. We put as the Ideal, service of the community of which he is a member, and for the sake of which he is to live and work. That is the entire difference—the opposite poles of being. That is the one which, in all ages, Prophets and Seers have declared, and the time has now come for its realisation. Now is the great opportunity, when the world has proved the failure of struggle and combat, has seen their end to be destruction, and is ripe to receive the message of peaceful and ordered advance, when law will no longer have for its object the mere prevention of injury to another, but will try to help forward the good of all, a positive not a negative endeavour to bring about the happiness of all. In fact the whole atmosphere is entirely changed. And let me say, as I spoke of the individualistic tendency of Christianity, that that was not the whole doctrine of the value of the individual; there was another doctrine shown out in the life of its

Founder, shown out in the teaching of the Christ, which was that when strength was attained it was to be used for service and not for tyranny. " The greatest among you," He said, " is he that doth serve "—not he that tries to force others into obedience unto his will, to work for his profit. That is the great teaching, the teaching of the service of the poor and the weak, that authority means helpfulness; that was the great legacy of the Christ to the world, and the inspiring motive held up to the believer in the Christ was, that though " He was rich, yet for our sakes He became poor, that we by His poverty might be made rich ". That was the life, that the example, which raised a very passion of devotion, and efforts to copy that self-sacrifice. That is one of the new motive powers in the world. If He did that for us, shall not we do the same for those who are weaker, more helpless than ourselves ? That was the last word of Christ, that the real heart of the teaching of the Christ, and that the great force of example, the very power of the Cross, of Christ as God incarnate. Mark well this deepest meaning of the Cross, the heart of the ancient pre-Christian Mysteries : Love crucified in the heart for the perfecting, the deification, of man. That conception of the perfecting of man will be the keynote of the coming civilisation. Service of the community will be the object, service of the larger, not the smaller, self. It is not enough to refrain from inflicting injury ; it is necessary to be active in promoting the happiness of our fellow-men.

Looking at that as the new basis, as the new Ideal, we must needs appeal to the highest in man and not to the lowest; but we can appeal with a perfect confidence in the success of that appeal. You can find that even among the roughest crowds. In a country like England where there are rougher people than here, you raise no enthusiasm at all if you describe the career of some man who by extra power of brain had been able to control the services of thousands of men, to fill his own pockets out of their toil, giving them back only a fraction of what they had produced. They will listen, they will wish to be among the lucky ones, those who plunder rather than those who are plundered; it does not move them to any enthusiasm. But if you tell them the story of any man who rushes into danger for the saving of another, if you tell them of a man who plunges into a torrent or a burning house, to save a woman who is drowning or is cut off by the flames, if you speak to them of a man who goes down into the pit to save some of his comrades, victims of a terrible explosion, then the whole crowd will rise as one man into wild enthusiasm over the courage and self-sacrifice which many of them might not be able to emulate. That is the first stage towards realising it in yourself. That is the voice of the God in you recognising the God in the hero. For where you are able to admire, there the desire to emulate wakes up in you, and the divine in you whispers that that is the road to true happiness, and not the gratification of the individual desires of a man. I have no fear of the result of the teaching which thus appeals to the greatest and noblest in man.

Now we come to ask another question : How is the authority of one man over another to be justified ? It was answered of old during the time we had Divine Kings, the noblest of rulers, all servants of man. They were greatest in wisdom, greatest in achievement, greatest in power of inspiration of others. The call of the God in them was answered by the infant God in the people, and they followed because the ruler was what they longed to be. Authority which is according to law is based on wisdom, character, and power to inspire by illuminating the intelligence and directing the emotions. All other authority is usurpation, no matter what the trappings. Such leaders of men are ever Kings ruling by the Grace of God, Kings by Divine Right. These are they after whom modern Democracy is groping, the way to find whom, and the way to put them in the Seats of Power, Democracy will one day discover. The counting of heads without regard to what they contain is emphatically not the way.

We have been getting wider and wider electorates in the West, time after time. What is called there

" reform " has been the enlargement of the electorate, and the extension of the suffrage has been held as the triumph of Democracy. After all the value of a head depends very much upon its content, and I have sometimes unkindly said that if you multiply nothing by a thousand there remains nothing at the end. These electorates determine difficult questions of commerce and industry, although the larger number of them do not know anything of production and distribution. They will elect legislators to deal with all questions, with the solution of which they are absolutely ignorant, and to which they are largely indifferent. The result is that one who has a sweet tongue wins his way, and a man who suits himself to the weaknesses and follies and prejudices of the people often gains their suffrages. I do not believe in that kind of Democracy. It is Democracy in its infancy. One day Democracy will find out its best men. The people long for happiness; they do not know how to obtain it. They know their object, but not the way to it. Wisdom and character must show the way, and power to inspire must induce the people to tread it. Every man has the right to go his own way, provided he wants nothing from anybody else. When he wants anything from Society, then certain obligations come in. If he is willing to live in a desert and asks nothing from anybody, then he ought to be allowed to live free, as he likes, but it is the characteristic of human nature to long to live

in Society and to develop best in it; and when they
recognise the right to rule in wisdom and in
character, then not by compulsion but by willing
acclamation they follow. Carlyle once said that men
need and desire a leader. There is a certain truth
in that. All men seek leading of some kind and
search for it, and find it sometimes in very curious
places. Every community will gladly follow the
man who serves it best, helps it to happiness and
to nobility of life; and so we come to see that
there are certain qualities in a man which make him
a leader of men, and people will follow his words and
advice.

When looking at leadership, we find that there is
much talk about it nowadays, and it is said that the
leader has to lead from behind, that is, that a leader
leads by following the people and not by going in
front, by staying behind, seeing in which way they
want to go, and leading them in that way. That is
fairly comfortable for the leader. It is easy. There
is no danger, no risk, no responsibility. But that is
not leadership. That is being a spokesman only, a
mouth, not a brain and a heart. If you take a great
crowd and say merely what they want, that is not
leading the crowd but only speaking what they want
to have. He has then often to depend upon the
opinion of the crowd, to change as it changes, to be
blown about by every breeze of popular passion and
prejudice. To my mind, a leader means a man of

insight and of devotion to the people's highest good, a man who sees a great Ideal before others see it, and is able to induce the people to see it through him, a man who sees far and sees truly, who understands men, and therefore is able to guide them. That is what leadership has always meant in the past. The leader is a man in whom God is manifest more than in the average man, and who appeals to that Highest in all. Such men may be found in any nation, any community, caste or class, and their divine right comes not by human gift, but by the recognition of their power to guide and rule and help; those are the true rulers, who can lead people into happiness through righteousness, because they have the vision of the Supreme, and can help their younger brothers to tread in the path of evolution. If they are much before their time, then they are generally persecuted, and in the savage times were burnt and tortured. If the people are nearer to them, they are apt at times to be rejected and ostracised; but they know what they have seen, they know what they are aiming at, and they wait until enough people see to make the realisation possible. A true leader is a Server of men, he who can serve best; and that means understanding, that means knowledge, that means experience, that means study and insight. If I am asked: Who is the best leader? my answer would be, the man who is the best Server, that is the man who can best lead the Nation on the highest path which it is able to tread. And what is his reward? Not power, not ease, not luxury, not money, but a greater opportunity to serve and a greater capacity to serve; that is the only reward worth having. For the Server is not seeking for himself, but helping the community of which he is a part, and that is the reason why leadership comes really by Divine Right, as they used to say of the Kings. For the Kings in the old days were men who served their people, and if you read about Indian Kings in the days of those Divine Kings, you will find that they were awake in order that others might sleep, they were toiling in order that others might enjoy. And if you take the histories of the East, you may read how they often found it difficult to secure a man even as governor of a province, because of the responsibility it entailed on the ruler. In those old days they used to blame the governor and not the people, if the people went wrong; the governor and not the subject, if the subject were unhappy. Once a King asked Confucius: "Why are there so many robbers in my land?" and his answer was: "If you yourself, O King, were not a robber, there would be no robbers among your subjects." That was the old way of answering. The greater the power the greater the responsibility, and it was carried out in such a practical way, as you probably have read, that if a man lost by theft the King's treasury had to pay fourfold the value of the man's stolen things; for it was held that it was the King and not the subject who had to suffer for the theft. That then is the qualification of a leader. He is the leader by wisdom, by character, by inspiration and by power.

Now, from what I have been saying about Democracy, you may suppose that I am not for wider electorates. But that is not so. I want power to be linked with knowledge, and not exercised by numbers only. Let me give you a brief outline for immediate use. I would give every man and woman of mature age in a village a vote in the government of the village, *i.e.*, a vote in the election of the Village Council, because they are the people to know exactly what the village wants, who know exactly the characters of the villagers, the grievances of the villagers, who know how they may be remedied ; and my universal suffrage would be for those who are living in a limited area, the wants and grievances of which they understand. That is what I want : to limit votes to dealing with things about which the voters have knowledge. Coming to a larger area, I want higher qualifications—better education, greater experience in service. And coming up to a district, larger knowledge, larger education and larger experience— and coming to the province still higher qualifications, and higher still for the Nation. That is : everyone would have one vote, and could win the additional votes in larger areas by knowledge and service. As an ordinary member of society, you go for your needs to the best man you can find and afford. You go to a man who understands his job. You do not go to a carpenter, and ask him to make an iron plough. You go for that to a blacksmith. It is not the carpenter's job. You suit the job to the capacity, and to the ability of the man who has to do it. In reorganising Society, you must see that all the functions of the Nation are discharged by the people who are best fitted for exercising the power which is placed in their hands, from the sweeper to the Head of the State. As I have often said, politics is the one subject in the world which, though it most affects the conditions and happiness of the people, is taken up by persons without any knowledge of it. You might as well set a shoeblack to navigate a ship; you would do less harm. You ought to understand how the welfare of the Nation depends upon, and is connected with, the welfare and the happiness of the communities which form the Nation. The men you send to Legislative Councils have to deal with education, with economics, with law and order, with agriculture, with the Nation's wealth and health and finance. How do you choose them? Do you demand sound knowledge on any one of these vital matters?

Now on industry I want to put to you one point. You know how you sometimes call the creation of the whole world the Līla of Īshvara, His play, His amusement, and every one of you takes pleasure in a thing you can do well. You like to create a thing that you can create well. It is a joy to you, not a toil. We have had many examples both here and in England. In the old Guild system, whether in India or in England it does not matter, the work of the craftsman was done admirably for the sake of, and the joy in, his work. He would shape a thing well, work it out regularly. He must do well what he did, and his joy and pride was in the perfection of the article that he created. He would add twists and twirls to make it more pleasant to the eye. How many of our workers to-day take joy and pride in their work. When the bell rings, down go the tools. You may say : " Yes, that is all true, but are you sure, if they started that system again, they would succeed ? " I say, yes. They have started that system again in England as an experiment in a small way. There are Building Guilds in England. Guilds of operative builders, masons, architects, all that are wanted for building houses, so that in your Guild you have men who produce a house. These men are not employed by contractors. They join together in their work to produce and finish a house. They make their own contracts before they begin. They are able to undersell the contractors, because they do not work for profit but for the service of the community, and the right to live by labour in that community. These were ordinary workers, but one of them not long ago said : " We

will give them such work as they never had before."
I believe this feeling and system will spread over
here also, because it is much more in consonance with
the Indian spirit than the spirit of competition, which
has been imported here in labour questions. That is
the work that I want some people to take up here,
who can really work it on sound business lines.
For it is not a charity, but a definite business under-
taking. And I would like some of our clever men to
work it out here in India, as they are working it out
in England, so that you can get rid of the horror of
unemployment, the hurry and the rush and the struggle of the modern life, and men may be their own
masters in their work. And I would revive that old joy
in industry, on a basis on which the craftsmen would be
proud of their work, and the world-wide distribution
of the products would be seen as a joy in bringing
the Nations together in co-operation and not in competition. The basis of production and distribution
will be " For use not for profit," and there lies the
solution of the problem of property and riches.
Land and capital for use, not for profit; the workman
working to produce for use and not for profit, to
make what is wanted, not create what is not wanted,
to produce according to the demand for the things
which they manufacture, and not to create a demand
to get rid of unwanted things. In that way the
whole life would be altered. You would have the
life of the community organised for Service.

In considering the relation of Law to Conscience, I would only briefly remind you that human law is but the expression of the stage of evolution at which average men have arrived; law is the embodied conscience of the majority. An individual with a conscience below the average is a criminal; an individual with a conscience above the average is at a higher stage of evolution, and is often a martyr. By his following of his conscience in a breach of law, he tends to raise the level of the social conscience, provided he unmurmuringly suffers the penalty by which respect for law is maintained for the ordinary man. Law-breaking merely as a definite defiance or flouting of authority by the breaking of a law which the conscience does not condemn is a serious crime against Society, for it encourages the criminal class, and strikes at the foundation of Society, which can only exist by a general respect for law.

The relation again of the Individual to the State is one of the highest importance. By "State" should be understood not the "Government" but the organised Nation, of which the Executive is the administrative agent. The Government is threefold: the Legislature which makes the laws; the Judiciary which interprets and applies the laws, whether at the instance of the citizen or of the Executive; the Executive, which administers National business, and protects the citizens by enforcing law and order. The Individual is a unit, a cell in the Body Politic.

The State is the environment into which he is born, and between himself and that environment there is continual interaction and mutual service; the State protects his life, liberty and property, surrounds him with all that separates him from the savage, gives him security, education, culture, all that raises man above the brute. In return, he owes it service, respect, obedience in all that his conscience does not forbid. Its interests are above his; its safety more important than his; to refuse to succour it is the most contemptible cowardice; to betray it is the foulest crime; to cheat it is the lowest meanness; to insult it is the gravest outrage. To be a good citizen is a man's highest duty; to be a bad citizen his lowest dishonour.[1]

Thus I submit for our basis for the solution of World Problems that the great principle we have to follow is that at our present stage in evolution man instinctively answers to and takes joy in the right, and not in the wrong; that his impulses are towards sacrifice more than towards selfishness; that the right to rule comes by wisdom, character and service, and the willingness to follow a leader comes from the recognition that he is able to lead towards a great Ideal, partly grasped by mind and heart, and inducing action.

---

[1] This paragraph and the preceding one are added, time not permitting me to deal with their content. I have written tersely the gist of what I intended to say, following in the first the principle I have laid down elsewhere, and in the second views that I have expressed more at length in other writings.

Without doubt, change is coming all around you; you can see the signs of it everywhere; your only choice is whether you will go back to the system which has broken down; or go back further still to that primitive condition from which you have emerged, renouncing all that you have gathered up in your age-long struggles and difficulties, the results of many generations of human dreamers, of human workers; or whether you will gather up all that has been gained, and go forward to your goal in the future. If you choose the last, then you must see if out of your past, with your intelligence and inspiration, you can plan out a specific basis of service, of duty to the community, of helping humanity. You already, in your family, sacrifice yourselves, those of you who are elders, in order that the youngers may profit by your sacrifice. How often fathers and mothers starve themselves to educate their children, and when their children grow up into manhood and womanhood, they follow your example, and they in their turn are ready to sacrifice themselves as fathers and mothers for their children. Now, I ask you to extend that same feeling, that same splendid spirit of sacrifice to the community around you, to the Nation around you; to give your best for the helping of the Nation, for the Nation is greater than any family, and even the future of the family depends upon the future of the Nation. Realise that this can only be done by common endeavour, by love, by drawing together, never by disintegration. That is the great task that lies before you; and let me say to you who are Indians, you can do it for the world better than any other Nation can do it. Your old Ideal of the State, your joint-family system, your Ideal of obligation, long built out of the family-ties, must extend to the larger families of the province, the Nation; your sense of duty, so abundant in Indian life, extend it to the State, and then to Humanity. These are the things that we want to revive, to strengthen; we want to widen them out, as Manu said: " Let all the elders be as your parents; let all your equals be as your brothers and sisters; let all the youngers be as your children," to be helped and guided. You have it all, but alas! you have forgotten. There is no Ideal more wonderful than the Ideal of old India, and a splendid practice that made that Ideal live in ordinary life. Oh! remember what your fathers thought and wrought with that Ideal before them. Remember the splendour of their literature, the beneficence of their political science, the knowledge with which they welded together the strengths and the weaknesses of humanity into the stablest civilisation that the world has ever known. The days of caste by birth are over; the days of vocation by quality, which is the very foundation of the caste system, are now upon us, and will again prevent the strife of warring classes. With the principle recognised, that each one has a particular vocation for some special work in the Nation, the

C

occupation of each of you will be decided by your faculty, by your power. There is no other Nation that has built on these foundations, which you have to build on, according to the old principles made into modern practice. Then let it be your destiny to work on this ancient-modern philosophy, and thus may you become the leader of the Nations of the World.

THEOSOPHY AND THE CULT OF BEAUTY

THE general plan of this course of Convention lectures was outlined yesterday by the President of the Theosophical Society. Each of us who comes after her is trying to fit himself, in the exposition of his particular subject, into the broad frame-work which she has given us. She explained yesterday what that frame-work is. It is for the Theosophical Society to give to the world certain great principles of action. Wherever the Theosophical Society goes, the Wisdom which it has to give deals essentially with action.

Now at the present epoch in the world's history, the President pointed out, there are great changes taking place. Because of these changes it is imperative, she told us, that we should have new motives, and that the world should go in a new direction. In discussing what that new motive and the new direction must be, she told us that we must take one guiding principle, as the illuminating truth in the knowledge of which alone we can find the solution to all problems. This principle is the Divinity in Man.

We shall be able to sum up all that is said in the lectures of this Convention in one phrase, " Deification of Man ". It is in the light of that truth that the only rational solution can be found—in political development, in economics, in education, in nationalism.

I shall therefore be visualising all the time that aim throughout what I am going to expound to you in my particular topic. But to make my topic more comprehensible to you, I must ask you to start with one great recognition, which does not deal at first with action but with knowledge. If we have right knowledge to start with, we shall be able to make our action utterly a success. Of all the great facts which have been discovered for us, and will be discovered, there is one fact which summarises, I think, all the others. It is that the universe is a releasing of a hidden Power. We are apt to think of the universe as some mechanical organism going on from age to age, somehow working out a destiny imposed upon it. Let us change that thought, and think of the universe as a storehouse of Power, as a casket within which is locked a splendid jewel.

Every kind of activity then, in every age, in natural or supernatural realms, is aimed at revealing more and more of the beauty of the casket, at releasing more and more Power from the secret recesses of the universe. It was said by Michael Angelo that " the more the marble wastes the more the statue grows ". In exactly the same way, every fraction of time that the universe exists, there is more Power being released, there is more Life, more Beauty. The mere existence of the universe as such is a process of releasing that which is within.

This process of the release of the hidden Power, Beauty, and Wisdom of the universe goes on by certain great stages. Of these stages, we are all familiar with one stage. It is that in which we live to-day. It is a stage of competition and combat. Now that too is a stage in the process of releasing; and however much combat and struggle, war and cruelty, are terrible evils, yet, because they are modes of the self-revelation of the universe, there is something inspiring even in their terror.

At each stage the Hidden Divinity reveals Himself according to His own "Word". It is for us to understand the laws of His revelation. In the stage of competition, we have, coming as a part of civilisation, man as the unit of the family, and the family as the unit of the nation. All such religions as have existed hitherto have subserved this great principle, by emphasising the relation of the individual to the family group, and of the family group to the nation. That is practically the position we are in to-day, except that there are changes evident. The world is always a "changing world," and that means that constantly new Power, new Wisdom, new Beauty are being released.

Now there is a process of release which has begun, and which to us, as Theosophists, is of the utmost fascination, for wherever God works there is wisdom. This new releasing of Power, Wisdom, and Beauty seems at first sight hardly a release at all. For to-day it looks as if all civilisation went backward instead of forward. That is because we are still under the force of the great materialistic ideas which began a century and a half ago. Practically the civilisation of all the most forceful nations, forceful at least so far as material changes are concerned, is still that of materialism. It is this materialistic civilisation which has brought about, as the President has pointed out, all the horrors which we have seen in the great War, and all the more frightful horrors which modern science promises to us in a future war.

Our present stage of upheaval, of intense discomfort, is a transition stage, and in a transition the ignorant man finds chaos, but the wise man sees the arising of a new order. Now what is this new order which is arising? It is arising very largely as the result of materialistic science. This science, which thinks of man merely by his outer garb, and sees nothing of Spirit in the universe, has brought about, as the work of its materialistic teaching, a curious unification among the nations. It has taught us that all men, of every race, of every epoch, are the descendants of common ancestors. of a brute creation

It has taught us that we have all a common destiny, which is death and extinction. All the differences which exist as between the East and the West, as between the cultured man and the ignorant man, are trivial in the light of evolution. Wè are as bubbles of foam in a great sea of evolution, and why should one bubble quarrel as to its size or colour with another bubble, since all the bubbles are so transitory ? In these latter days especially, we are all being surrounded with terror. For science is arming each one of us with death-dealing forces, so that, unless we assert the nobility inherent in us, there is every inducement offered us to behave as the brute and not as the man.

Yet in spite of all these disadvantages which science brings us, there are certain advantages which every thoughtful man can see. They consist in the linking together of cultures, of nations, by means of the telegraph, the printing-press, and the steamer. I hold that no man or woman can now be a representative of the best of his land, unless he has enlarged the boundaries of his national life, and livès, in some part of his life, in the other nations of the world. It is this large thought of the world which science has given us. Of course every religion, every philosophy, has that fundamental thought of the Totality of which we are parts ; but that idea of the Whole has been hitherto restricted to mystic and philosophical schools. But ·to-day, there it is, and in every newspaper is now reflected something of a world problem, of a world destiny. We talk now of the "world's needs". These very lectures are based upon that new conception, the relation which Theosophy bears to "world problems".

Because there does now exist the thought of a world destiny, there is therefore a new conscience in the world. This new conscience is as yet feeble, but it is trying to express itself to-day at the Disarmament Conference in Washington; it is trying to speak out its message in the deliberations of the League of Nations. All of us here in India are removed by thousands of miles from Washington, and yet we are parts of that world conscience there, which is at this present moment struggling to make itself heard.

It is a characteristic, then, of the world as it is to-day, that there is something new which did not exist before. That is why the President pointed out that every problem must be seen from a new direction, and that new motives must be brought out of men's lives in order to fulfil the new need. Now the duty of the Divine Wisdom is always to lead in clear ideas and principles, and it is interesting here to note that before the world conscience was born, before this pressing world need arose, our Theosophical Society was sent forty-six years ago into the world, by the great Guardians of Humanity, in order to fulfil just this world need of to-day. From the day that the Society was formed, great fundamental ideas have been offered to the world stage by stage, so that the world might understand, for what the world requires first is understanding.

What is the first idea which was offered ?

It is that Brotherhood is a fact, not an ideal to aim at, like some possible realisation of the dreams of poets, but a living Fact, as much a part of Nature as is gravity. We have been trying to proclaim to the world that the right and wrong of individual conduct, or of national policy, must be weighed only in the balance of this great truth of Universal Brotherhood. That was the first great ideal which we gave, to be as a guiding clue to all who care to understand what is right policy in individual and collective action. The second great idea which we gave was that there is a Path to Deification open, even in these materialistic days, as it has been open from the beginning. of time. We showed that Mysticism was the real living source of religion, and that he who is a Mystic inevitably finds that his experience comes at his own first hand, and not through a tradition. We have proclaimed the existence of the great Masters of Wisdom, those Elder Brothers of the human race who ever stand to teach and guide the world. So, stage by stage, going several generations in advance of humanity, this Theosophical movement has given ideas, which those who seek to understand find as great illuminating pointers.

The next great idea was that all the activities of men are directed by a Hierarchy of perfected beings, who are the rulers of men as They are the servants of God. It is this great thought which in these days we crystallise in the phrase "the Divine Plan". It is startling to the modern enquirer to be told, when he surveys the chaos of the world, when he sees its cataclysms, its six years' War, that behind them all is a Divine Plan. And yet that is the statement we are making, and we are emphasising it to-day to all who care to listen to us. In our teachings as to the Divine Plan, we point out that nothing happens by chance, that there is a plan for every nation, as, too, for the whole world. We have been teaching for long that there was always a plan for the individual's life. We called it Karma. We teach now that there is a plan for each nation too, and for the whole world also.

Theosophy, then has, stage by stage, offered great guiding principles. It is these guiding principles which it is our mission to give to the world. I hold that in many ways we should be wasting something of our force, if we were, as a Society, to throw ourselves wholly into the world of action. There are thousands who will rush into action; too few who will stay a while to inquire whether there is a Wisdom, in the light of which men should act so as to bring about the best action. That is the mission of our Society, which stands first and foremost for the Divine

Wisdom—to be the expounders of the great principles of the future, as age by age those principles are required by the changing world.

Now I am going to deal this afternoon with a principle which will help us to understand a little bit more what is the working of the Divine Plan. This principle is nothing new; it exists in all the great philosophies. It is that the Universe is one living Whole. We are taught in modern science that the tiniest atom is linked to the mightiest solar system by a community of matter and force. We note in psychology that the germ of consciousness in the smallest living organism is linked to the mightiest intellect of man. But we have yet to realise that when we say the "universe," it is something instinct with mind, throbbing with love, charged with idealism. When we look at this Shamiana, [1] at these posts which are so still, it is difficult for us to understand, to realise, that in the matter of each post is a consciousness which is thinking, loving, striving, glorying in the fact of its existence, and planning to reveal itself more and more in its beauty. We go through the universe as if it were dead and we only were alive, whereas the contrary is so much more the truth. It is the world which is living, it is the air which is throbbing with idealism, it is we who are dead. If only we could come to that first fundamental fact, that each speck of matter in every moment of time is a

[1] The decorated tent in which the lecture was given.

container of idealism, of hopes and dreams, of joys and endeavours, of a perfect Wisdom, of an omnipotent Power, then we should understand what the Universe is living and working for. Suppose for a moment we were to begin to have a dim realisation of what I mean by this phrase " the living universe," then we should know that what the universe is doing all the time is pressing forward to Unity. All the time, there is this inner urge to bring substance, thought, feeling, to one great Unity. Call that Unity God, call it Eternal Law, call it Brahman ; names little matter. They conceal the Fact of Facts.

Ekam saṭ viprāh bahudhā vaḍanṭi ;
Agnim, Yaman, Māṭarishvānam āhu :

By many names the Sages speak of the One Existence ;
They call IT Agni, or Yama, or Māṭarishvān.

Little matters what the name is, but the Fact is there, so overwhelming in its magnificence that the mightiest intellect bows down with utmost awe and reverence, and yet also with supreme hope and joy.

This Totality, then, is bringing everything to realise that Fact. The whole world is one centripetal force, though it uses many subsidiary forces to bring all together. We see those forces already at work in humanity. Of these, one, perhaps the oldest, is religion. In that aspect of religion which is Mysticism, you will find that this predominating characteristic of the universe is fully realised. Mysticism ever brings to a centre. The Mystic of the East is the same as the Mystic of the West. Wherever a man transcends the outer form of religion and creed, and comes to the heart of his own faith, he is the Mystic. He then salutes as a brother in the spiritual life the Mystic of every other creed.

Not less is all this true of Science. The highest science unites. The discoveries of the greatest scientists are not characterised by any nationality or age. Because of that ideal characteristic of science, all the greatest scientists reverence each other, because they are the discoverers and expounders of one common Wisdom. Science is a unifying force. It has its aspects of destruction, but that is science as it is wrongly applied by human nature. But pure science unifies.

We have in the world to-day another force which is also unifying us. It is a factor which is not limited to religious people, though it has so many of the characteristics of religion. I mean Humanitarianism. There are thousands of men and women who do not care to identify themselves with any religion, and yet who take as their religion the great gospel of human suffering and its abolition. The humanitarian, whether he is of the East or of the West, salutes as brothers in a common endeavour all humanitarians of every nationality.

There are many such unifying forces already; many more will come, as the universe releases itself more and more.

Now it is the duty of Theosophists, with the wisdom which illuminates every problem, to grasp these unifying forces and to intensify them. The fascination of Theosophy to the Theosophist lies in the fact that he sees ahead ; and however much his hands may be feeble to accomplish, at least he can do this much for his better equipped fellows : he can point to them the way along which they can rightly go.

Our duty therefore is to intensify these unifying forces. Each force unifies by releasing more and more of the true nature of the universe. There is more Beauty, more of God's Life, in the world, because religion has come ; and there is more of God's Power in the world because modern science has been born. Wherever there is some new force driving to unity, the universe is more powerful, and that means every one of us can achieve his destiny the sooner. Now there is to-day one new force among men which is building new bonds; it is that force which underlies the Cult of Beauty. My interest in explaining the subject of Beauty to you is to point out in what way we Theosophists are called upon to carry on the message of this new and great unifying force.

All the time, I am thinking of Beauty as a unifying force in the world ; and how because of that characteristic, it releases more Power, Love, Wisdom and Beauty in the universe. Most of us think of beauty usually as a heavenly manna to feed our individual selves. We train ourselves to appreciate beauty, because it brings *us* to happiness. But we have not yet realised beauty as a great principle of the universe. That is the next stage into which some of us now, all of us some day, must pass, if we are to help in the great work of the releasing of the powers of the universe.

This recognition of beauty as a bond has yet to come. It came in a fragmentary way in Greece, where beauty was recognised as a principle of statecraft. For the first time probably in humanity, the little States of Greece, and especially Athens, took as a guiding principle of State development that beauty should enter into the lives of the individuals of the State. Because of that, we have an epoch in history which stands out still with living light though ages have passed. To every one who tries to understand the Cult of Beauty, there is inevitably a need to understand what the Greeks meant by beauty, for the Greeks made beauty a vital thing. So much was it a living thing in the life of the city of Athens, that life was transformed in a way that we cannot understand to-day, for beauty is a gospel to which we have yet to commit our faith. To the Greek, it was not a mere gospel, it was something that the men of Athens *lived*, not merely dreamed of. They tell the story of a Spartan who came from outside Athens and saw the city and its inhabitants. When he went back, he was asked about his experiences of Athens, and he described it in one laconic phrase: " Athens! All things noble there!" In that statement he brought out the salient fact that in Athens there were new values to all things, and that all men and things had a nobility revealed in Athens which was hidden in Sparta.

Now it is this "new value to all things" which we have to realise from the Cult of Beauty. This Cult of Beauty as a principle of the State began practically with Athens. It has been since slowly developed, specially in Italy in the Middle Ages. It has now spread from land to land, and it is that marked characteristic which I want to point out to you. It is a unifying force. The empire of Art is very, very small as yet, but it has certain characteristics, and of these the first is that Art, or the Cult of Beauty overrides nationality. It has been very truly said that Art knows no fatherland. Now that does not mean that an artist may not be an ardent patriot. But if he is the true artist, he is all the time trying to see through particulars into universals; in other words, consciously or unconsciously in his artistic creation, he is looking through his art as through a window into a larger world, and this larger world is not of his nation, and not of his age, but of all times, and of all peoples.

This characteristic is to be found wherever there is any true artistic creation. The poems and plays of Tagore, the pictures of the "Calcutta school," the statues and carvings in various places in India, are felt at once in the West as having a message to the West also. Each of these speaks of a universal Cult, and the artist of the West treasures the art of the East, because, while it may have particular Eastern characteristics, yet in truth it has no characteristic of one sole fatherland. We can take the pictures of Japan, or read their striking "Nō" plays, and through each of them we can look into a larger world. Art is a world of beauty, and it little matters to us whether the window into that world is built from the East or from the West, so long as we look out of our world and see another which is but dimly reflected in this our drab workaday world.

Artists, therefore, have, if they are truly artists, a curious quality of bringing people to people. Artists also have one other characteristic, and that is, they are all brothers. When the artist of the West meets the artist of the East, they meet as brothers. They are fellow-worshippers at one shrine, workers in one divine workshop. Now wherever there is any principle which works for Brotherhood, we have the emphasising of the centripetal force which drives to a Unity. It is because of that, that I have taken this subject of the Cult of Beauty as one of the developable principles in human life, by which the great Plan of God may be revealed the sooner.

There is then a principle of Beauty at which the artists are trying to come; it drives to Unity. The moment you see even intellectually this true principle

D

underlying beauty, you are driven from within you to come to the centre, you are driven by your own conscience to work for others sooner or later. As you go to the centre and grasp the principle of beauty, you cannot be a disuniter, you must become a harmoniser.

But it is not easy to grasp the principle of beauty. Indeed there is the greatest danger in misunderstanding what beauty is. It requires a very great presumption on the part of any one to lay down what are all the true principles underlying this great subject of beauty. Yet I think a Theosophist may presume a great deal because, when he approaches any one problem, he has behind him some general conception of all the problems. A Theosophist works from the centre, and because of that, if he is a careful student and an earnest aspirant, he is on the whole more likely to hit the truth and not the falsehood.

In trying to understand the principle of beauty, the first thing which occurs to me is this : beauty is not in the thing which we call beautiful, but in the *idea* about the thing. Now that is not an easy conception to grasp, but in order to get you to follow my thought, let me read to you here a little poem, " The Toys," of Coventry Patmore :

> My little Son, who look'd from thoughtful eyes
> And moved and spoke in quiet grown-up wise,
> Having my law the seventh time disobeyed,
> I struck him and dismissed
> With hard words and unkiss'd.

His Mother, who was patient, being dead.
Then, fearing lest his grief should hinder sleep,
I visited his bed,
But found him slumbering deep,
With darken'd eyelids, and their lashes yet
From his late sobbing wet.
And I, with moan,
Kissing away his tears, left others of my own;
For, on a table drawn beside his head,
He had put, within his reach,
A box of counters and a red-vein'd stone,
A piece of glass abraded by the beach,
And six or seven shells,
A bottle with bluebells
And two French copper coins, ranged there with
    careful art,
To comfort his sad heart.
So when that night I pray'd
To God, I wept and said:
Ah, when at last we lie with trancèd breath,
Not vexing Thee in death,
And Thou rememberest of what toys
We made our joys,
How weakly understood
Thy great commanded good,
Then, fatherly, not less
Than I whom Thou hast moulded from the clay,
Thou'lt leave Thy wrath, and say,
" I will be sorry for their childishness."

What was it that influenced the little boy so
profoundly, so that his emotional nature was changed
slowly from one of grief to one of consolation? It
could not surely be the little objects, in their mere
appearance. What is there in

A box of counters and a red-vein'd stone,
A piece of glass abraded by the beach,
And six or seven shells.

A bottle with bluebells,
And two French copper coins,

to produce that great change? It is obvious that
what did produce the change was the thought about
these trivial things. It was in the thought about
them that he found in some mysterious way the arms
of his dead mother round him.

That is exactly the case with regard to all that we
call beauty. Beauty is not in the hand, in the face,
in nature, but it resides in the superimposed idea.

Of course, it is true that, with regard to everything
which consciousness can cognise, there is always an
idea imposed on every object. But the conception of
beauty resides in the idea, and not in the thing which
we call beautiful. I want to make this point clear,
because, without an understanding of it, my further
remarks will not be intelligible. Because beauty
resides in the idea, and not in the substance, we find
an explanation of the contradictory attitudes of
people; one man will say that a face to him is
beautiful, while another will flatly contradict him.

Consider too how, to one with artistic sensitive-
ness, beauty is being created all the time in a way
that does not happen to others. If an ordinary
individual and an artist are travelling in a train, the
artist, as he looks out, will see, in the rearrangement
of trees and shrubs, lines and colours of the land-
scape, as the train moves, picture after picture. In
other words, to him the moving world is all the time

" composing " pictures. To the great musician, melodies and symphonies are being woven, as he listens to the sounds round him; the murmur of forest leaves is beautiful to him, because it is translated in his consciousness in terms of music.

So the whole universe is Brahman, as we say here. There is always an underlying Unity. When we exercise our rational nature, we find this Unity at once, and it comes from within our nature and not from without. Futhermore, when we see in that Unity the vision of Beauty, that vision does not arise from the thing itself, except by way of reflection from it. We call a thing beautiful, because the Beauty Maker is everywhere, and it is His thought reflected on to the object which then evokes in us a similar thought. Who is the Maker of Beauty is most deeply suggested by the great Sufi Poet, Jāmi.

> In solitude, where Being signless dwelt,
> And all the universe still dormant lay
> Concealed in selflessness, One Being was,
> Exempt from " I " or " Thou "-ness, and apart
> From all duality ; Beauty Supreme,
> Unmanifest, except unto Itself
> By Its own light, yet fraught with power to charm
> The souls of all ; concealed in the Unseen,
> An Essence pure, unstained by aught of ill.

> *   *   *   *   *

> Each speck of matter did He constitute
> A mirror, causing each one to reflect
> The beauty of His visage. From the rose
> Flashed forth His beauty, and the nightingale
> Beholding it, loved madly. From that fire

The candle drew the lustre which beguiles
The moth to immolation.   On the sun
His beauty shone, and straightway from the wave
The lotus reared its head.   Each shining lock
Of Leyla's hair attracted Majnun's heart,
Because some ray divine reflected shone
In her fair face.   'Twas He to Shirin's lips
Who lent that sweetness which had power to steal
The heart from Parviz, and from Farhad life.
His Beauty everywhere doth show itself,
And through the forms of earthly beauties shines
Obscured as through a veil.   He did reveal
His face through Joseph's coat, and so destroyed
Zuleykha's peace.   Where'er thou seest a veil,
Beneath that veil He hides.   Whatever heart
Doth yield to love, He charms it.   In His love
The heart hath life.   Longing for Him, the soul
Hath victory.   That heart which seems to love
The fair ones of this world loves Him alone.
Beware! say not: "He is All-Beautiful,
And we His lovers!" Thou art but the glass,
And He the face confronting it, which casts
Its image in the mirror.   He alone
Is manifest, and Thou in truth art hid.
Pure love, like beauty, coming but from Him
Reveals itself in thee.   If steadfastly
Thou canst regard, thou wilt at length perceive
He is the mirror also; He alike
The Treasure and the Casket.   "I" and "Thou"
Have here no place, and are but phantasies
Vain and unreal.   Silence! For this tale
Is endless, and no eloquence hath power
To speak of Him.   'Tis best for us to love
And suffer silently, being as naught.

This Beauty Maker is ever at work.   He is in every
speck of matter, in every point in space; He is
eternally weaving order out of chaos.   He is making
the cosmos from good to better, from better to best.

He is all the time weaving order. This is the Sanātana Dhamma which Lord Buddha proclaimed, that Law "eternal in the heavens," according to which the heart of man is built. It is the order of the universe, and this order is ever being emphasised in the changing world. He is Īshvara, the Lord, who establishes law after law, eternally emphasising the ancient order, yet multiplying laws, modifying them, to suit the needs of the changing world.

Out of each fact, out of each of us, He is distilling wisdom. For God, the eternal Thinker, though He is the root of all wisdom, yet is He all the time fashioning, for every moment, for every point in His space, the wisdom for that point, for that fragment of time. That is why He knows all that which is to be, not only the past and the present; He can tell us all that is going to be, without in the least infringing our free wills, for He sees the drift of each will, He sees the ultimate resultant of all the wills at work, the changing resultant each second, as our initiatives change the "parallelogram of forces". He is the fashioner of beauty, for, as He sees this changing world, He sees all the threads in its weaving as they break or come together. So the "heavenly carpet" is woven before His eyes. To Him, the universe is a revelation of beauty. This is what we have to realise, that the universe is creating beauty each fragment of time. His Beauty shines even from each little leaf and twig, that growing beauty which the universe creates every

instant.   It is that fact which we have given to us in
the *Gītā*, though so few have grasped in it this particular message :

> Among the Litanies I am the Bṛhaṭ Sāman, of the
> metres the Gāyatri.   .   .   .   Among the months, I am
> Mārgashīrsha.   Of all the seasons, I am the Spring.[1]

He is the Spring, because in all the roses, in all the
new leaves, in the cries of the birds, He, the Eternal
Maker of Beauty, is living, is seeing beauty, fashioning
beauty, and whoso cares to lift up his eyes can see.
The Maker of Beauty is all the time watching, and
giving His judgment.   He has before Him the great
Plan of ultimate perfection ; He knows that the
present moment is not the the perfect moment ; He
judges each thing that happens according to its
nearness to the final glory.   He sees each object as
less or more beautiful to Him, as it reflects less or
more of His Plan and His Beauty.

Thence follows a great principle of action, and it is
this : that this wondrous Beauty, which is universal, is
in man. I have said that our great principle throughout these lectures is the Deification of Man, and that
all problems must be considered from the standpoint
that within man is God, within man is the Whole.
Following this principle, it is only the next step to
realise that the beauty of the universe is in man's own
heart.   It is difficult for us, I know, in this world of
shadows, where we are groping in the dark, where

[1] Chapter X.

we have tried and failed to realise that the Power of
God is in us, that the Beauty of the universe is
enshrined in our own hearts. Yet we are not true
seekers of Wisdom until we start with the faith that,
however much the ugliness in us denies it, there is in
reality in our own heart a great beauty. If I see an
object as beautiful, it is partly because the great
Beauty Maker flashes to me His thought of that
particular beauty, and partly because He flashes
through me and imposes the idea of loveliness upon
the object before my eyes. So truly says Omar :

> The idol said to the idolator, " O my servant,
> Knowest thou for what reason thou hast become mine
>   adorer ?
> On me hath shone in his beauty that ONE
> Who looketh forth from thee, O my beholder ! "

Coming back to my main theme, it is surely well
that we should all recognise beauty. But that is not
enough ; we must create beauty as well, for the
universe is striving for perfection. God is a prisoner
in chains, and it is we who are to release Him. God
is the statue within the block of marble, and it is
we who must cut and carve with mallet and chisel, and
release the statue. And we release Him by identify-
ing ourselves with all the many types of unifying
forces ; and of these, one powerful force is beauty.

So we must create beauty, and thus bring the
universe to perfection. We are, as a matter of fact,
fashioners all the time ; not the youngest child but is

changing by the fact of his existence the nature of the universe. But each of us must understand that our desire, our aspiration, is swinging the universe to the right or to the left, onwards or away from the path. We are fashioning, making and unmaking ; but as we fashion, the great Beauty Maker must fashion through us.

The great principle for our daily life is so to live that while as brothers, we work for Wisdom, Internationalism, for all ideals, we are on the look out for new ways which will bring the world together. One of these new ways is the Cult of Beauty. To help in that, we must make beauty an active principle of our lives. But not for our sakes ; for if we see beauty from that standpoint of self-culture, of our happiness, nay, even of our own purification, we shall be led into many a temptation, and often to err grievously. But if we can make our motive pure, then our path will be without pitfalls. In the search of beauty, we must recognise that we must be pure for the world's sake, not in order that we may enjoy the blessings of purity.

My main interest in delivering this lecture is to emphasise the relation which beauty has to the world's welfare. Now that out of all lips there is a great cry, "Let us be one," and statesmen and economists and religious teachers and others are all striving to achieve a great Unity, let us help in it by throwing into the great centripetal forces the new force of

Beauty. For wherever Beauty is recognised, there Brotherhood inevitably results. For, as I have mentioned, beauty transcends the limitations of nationality, and the artist is a brother to every artist in the world.

When each one of us is able to create something artistic, then he is a living example of Brotherhood. He is then nearer to his brother, because he is not only living the gospel of Brotherhood but he is also creating artistically. But can all of us create artistically? Why not? The eternal Fashioner of Beauty is in us; and you will find as a matter of fact that, if you understand rightly the Wisdom which Theosophy brings you, you cannot help creating artistically. For instance, suppose as a student of Theosophy you seek to understand the great Wisdom not from ulterior motives, not for self, but simply because it is the great Wisdom, then you will inevitably find that the gospel of beauty becomes clearer to you day by day. Nay, the very key to Theosophy is its supremely beautiful and philosophical conception of the world. This vast structure of ideal principles, which we work out in our studies, is like a magnificent treasure-house of beauty. If you have an ideal of wisdom, then beauty flows from that ideal. Wisdom will teach you to contemplate life with compassion. Look at the common tragedy of men and give of your self to each suffering fellow-man, or animal, or plant, and you will find that beauty comes to you mysteriously, and you will see it, feel it, in even a blade of grass. You will find that as you sacrifice every fragment of yourself before the altar of the Great Self, beauty pours into you. For Beauty is the Great Self, as Beauty is also wisdom and compassion.

In all ways, each one of us by the mere fact of living can create beauty, if only we know how to create, that is how to live wisely. You cannot help creating beautiful thoughts if you are a Theosophist. Some beauty flashes from your face to your brothers, because you go about the world trying to feel Brotherhood; there is more wisdom radiating from your countenance, because you have recognised the Unity. Then we shall be as once of old in India, when as a man knew the Unity, it was said of him: " Your face shines like one who has seen Brahman. Who has taught you ?" Our faces will truly so shine, if only we understand the great truths of Theosophy, for to understand Theosophy is to begin to realise Brahman. Look round you then; if you have only eyes to see, the great Beauty Maker is for you everywhere. The artist sees in every line a beauty, in every shadow a light. Now India is specially the land where there are so many thousands of beautiful things, and you can see them all, if only you could train your eyes to see. If only we could see more clearly, life would be far easier to live ! There are everywhere here little things of beauty, and thousands of them are being created each day. Can you not imagine how from out of this little clay pot, made for menial use, which I found in my bath-room here, there comes to me a great thought about God,

because it is beautiful? It has an exquisite shape, though six can be bought for one anna, and as I contemplate it Theosophy is poured into me from that little clay vessel. And I know that in the potter, ignorant about many things about which I am wise, there is some wisdom for me. And so is it with all things. Wherever you find beauty, there is wisdom.

This, my brothers, is one part of our work, to help the world to become one. I know quite well that as we Theosophists speak of these high ideals, the world criticises us, because we fail to live them. Never mind the failure; we are the precursors of our greater selves which will some day achieve. At any rate let us tread the way, and show that, even though our lot may be to fail, we will ever try to succeed for the sake of the world. We are all under a very hard destiny, because we needs must talk of ideals, though we find that there is not enough strength in us to live them. Yet must we try to live them, remembering that "the more the marble wastes the more the statue grows" In our struggles, in our sufferings, the Divinity within us is being realised by us. We Theosophists must speak to the world, however little we may be able to bring about the fulfilment of the Great Plan by ourselves alone. In this year 1921, we must speak of the world as it shall be in the year 2,000, or even the year 20,000, for we are idealistic dreamers who are going to model the world into what it should be. Our hardships come from this fact, that we offer to become quickly what we seek. Though to become what we seek is hard, we must not renounce the search. We must go on seeking the signs of the perfected world, until the whole world reflects the great Beauty of God.

There is for us as Theosophists a very high privilege, which is to transcend the barriers which exist in the world, and to tell the world that there is for it a common destiny. Let us pin our faith to it, and let us speak of it, for each time we speak of it, we shall gain a little more strength to live it. For an ideal which I place before me, which I proclaim, that ideal is drawing me too, and giving me force. At least let me not fail in seeing my ideal.

So I dream of a world when the great Life of God shall be manifest in every home, in each street of each town, and God shall be there not only as Compassion, not only as Wisdom, but also as an indescribable Beauty.

———

THEOSOPHY AND INTERNATIONALISM

THEOSOPHY points out to us, and teaches, that all paths lead but to one God. It teaches us, whether we be Christians, Hindūs, Muhammadans or Buddhists, that to what religion we belong does not matter, that God is in essence eternally and perpetually the same, although He expresses Himself in all forms of belief and worship. A Nation is the expression of individuals, and individuals are the embodiment of the Divine. Consequently all Nations, whatever colour and degree of evolution they represent, are one in their divine essence. Thus we should imagine that every thinking man and woman would be an Internationalist. Unfortunately, this is not the case, as is shown by the innumerable wars which take place, and by the continuous strife and competition existing in every department of life. This has been caused by the lack of true feeling and deep thinking with regard to all the real problems of life, problems of vital importance, because they concern the life and happiness of every human being. We do not feel truly, because we have not acquired the power of putting ourselves in the place of other people ; we dare not think deeply, because such thoughts must bring about change, and we are afraid of change, lest it should cause us suffering.

We Theosophists have got to play a large part in the reconstruction of the world, and to this end we must learn both to think and to feel in a new way. The keynote of the New Age is Internationalism. What are the obstacles which at present stand in the way of realising this ideal ?

There are four fundamental questions which, more than anything else, influence the thought, the character and action of men. These are Education, Religion, Business, Patriotism. Let us examine these through the eyes of a real Theosophist. But let me first define what I mean by a real Theosophist.

We can all talk of Theosophy in high-sounding terms; can read and discuss its philosophy; but how many of us can act and live Theosophy in the ordinary commonplace things of daily life ? We *know* what we should be, and yet, like all other human beings, we are too feeble to carry out that knowledge. We lack the essential thing, which is the *will* to overcome all obstacles, and to live the things we know to be true. So by a real Theosophist, I mean one who *lives* Theosophy and does not merely talk about it.

Now what should be the Theosophical attitude towards the four subjects I have mentioned ? Let us first examine Education. True education must teach self-respect, the realisation of our own inner greatness.

E

How does the education existing in the world to-day
help to realise this ideal? First take a typical case of
an educated man in the West. I have in my mind a
friend of mine in England, a man who has followed
the usual course of education of an English
gentleman. He has been to a Preparatory School,
then to a Public School and, finally, to Woolwich. Woolwich is a Training College for officers,
where they turn out the regular type of young
soldier, who goes to India and to other parts
of the world to assist in building an Empire. Kipling
would hail my friend as the ideal Englishman and
Empire-Builder. He is clean and nice-looking, wears
well-cut clothes, is straight and honest, polite and
suave, a good friend, with a high opinion of his own
merits. The kind of self-respect which he has learnt
from his education is to regard himself as superior to
the men of all other races. Now let us examine him
from the standpoint of Theosophy.

His ideas are narrow and limited, in spite of the
fact that he has read many books and has passed
many examinations. He is incapable of grasping a
big international idea, or of looking at any question
except from an English point of view. I have often
tried to make him understand what an Indian feels
in being ruled over by another Nation, and when I
have tried to explain to him that it was a degradation
for any Nation to submit to foreign rule, his answer
was: "My dear fellow, we do you good!" He was

incapable of looking at life through my eyes, through my consciousness. This lack of imagination, of the power of putting himself in another man's shoes, is very characteristic of the Englishman. Evils must be brought right under his nose before he will try to remedy them, and he seems incapable of using the creative power of the imagination to picture conditions which he has not seen.

To return to my friend, he would call himself highly civilised; yet his chief purpose in life is to enjoy himself, to have a good time. In seeking his enjoyment, he does not consciously wish to hurt anybody, and would probably be very much surprised if you told him that by his enjoyment he causes suffering to other people. He is incapable of realising that by his selfishness, by his contentment with the littlenesses of life, by his small conception of happiness, he is directly injuring his fellow-men. The savage in Africa has the same desire—enjoyment, but he is more honest and simple in his selfishness. He says quite openly: " I desire such and such a pleasure, and I mean to gratify my desire, no matter who suffers." My friend would not express his feeling so crudely, but the result of his life upon his fellow-men is much the same as that of the savage. Western education has produced superficially good manners, and a covering of literary and artistic expression, but it has not in any way changed the real man within. He remains as crude in his ideals, as narrow and selfish in his outlook, as the uncivilised man. This kind of education forbids the realisation of any real spirit of Internationalism. It makes for limitation and narrowness of outlook, and does not sufficiently cultivate the imagination.

Now let us examine our Indian education through the eyes of the Theosophist. I wish to consider this subject quite impersonally, and therefore I may have to say some things which are not pleasing to my audience; but if we are going to change conditions, we must be prepared to hear the truth, even if it pains us. Let us take an average Indian student. The first impression that he makes upon us is that he is gentle, modest and obedient in the presence of his elders. When an older man speaks, the student listens and accepts unquestioningly. The spirit of the young Indian has been so long suppressed by his elders and by the ruling race, that his self-respect has become submerged almost to the point of disappearance. The life of the Indian student has been largely limited within the four walls of his school and college—his sole aim and ambition being to obtain a post as clerk in an office. The creative spirit, which is divine, has largely been crushed out of us, but now with a new awakening of National consciousness and self-respect, the student is adopting an aggressive rudeness towards superiors, equals and inferiors alike. It does not so greatly matter if we are rude to our superiors, because it

merely shows us to be fools. If we are aggressive
and rude to our equals, they retaliate and hit us back.
But to be aggressive and rude to our inferiors, is, to
my mind, passing the limits of decency. Even
Theosophists, I am sorry to say, are guilty of this
rudeness, and some of them treat their servants in
the most extraordinary manner. The other day
I met a servant whom I had known in England, and
naturally I shook hands with him when I saw him
here. People looked as surprised at this action, as if
it had lowered my self-respect. They failed to realise
that self-respect exists only in the man who respects
himself, and is ready to respect others. Rudeness is
no mark of self-respect, but the reverse. In India
we need to cultivate the spirit of adventure, and to
show manly strength and courage, while retaining our
tradition of courtesy and gentleness.

If we are to bring about true Internationalism, we
must change education both in the West and in the
East. We must take all that is best in the West and
not despise it, as we do at present; and we must
transplant all that is best in the East to the West.
Western people must cultivate something of that
gentleness which characterises the Indian, and both
East and West will need more imagination, if they
are to bring about great changes in the world.
Western people are full of energy, and if they could
add imagination to their energy, they would accomplish wonderful things. We must also transplant

compassion; not the compassion of a mother to her child, but the compassion that understands all and forgives all. From the West we must learn independence, the power to stand against the crowd that disagrees with us, which is opposed to us in every ideal, in every conception. Another thing which we lack most sadly in India is *esprit de corps*, which means co-operation. We can all co-operate with what we like; we must learn to co-operate with what we do not like, to put our little feelings aside when the good of the whole is involved. In an English public school the spirit of co-operation is dominant. If a few boys fight in the morning, their private quarrel is forgotten in the field in the afternoon, when they are playing for the honour of the school. Then they are one. We lack that spirit. We let our feelings interfere with the duties of life. We cannot afford to neglect the things which western people can teach us. We should not despise them, as we do at present, because they have a white skin. They cannot help being white, and some day we may also be born into a white-skinned Nation. If India is meant to do great things in the world, she must have control of all the forces which make for progress. I would suggest that one method by which this Internationalism could be brought about, would be the establishment of colleges all over the world, which would exchange students with the National schools and colleges of other countries, and thus create international relations between the young.

Thus young people would be properly trained to hold these larger ideas. First establish the spirit of goodwill, and then send Indian students abroad and take western students into your Indian schools.

We must also teach history in the schools so as to promote admiration for the good points of other Nations, and their special characteristics. Nowadays history is a record of wars, in which one Nation beats the other, and there is always the superior race dominating and the inferior race suffering. That is history as it is understood at present. In certain historical books, naturally, the other spirit, which presents the right attitude, is also represented, but unfortunately they are in a minority.

Now let us take up my second subject—Religion. That is the point on which I feel most strongly, and if I exaggerate, as I said before, it is because I want to kill what should be killed, as well as to create and heal. Religion should teach the right international spirit, but at present while it teaches us the right attitude towards God, it does not, unfortunately, teach us the right attitude towards our brother. Men treat those who are below them, or who are of a different colour or caste, or who hold different opinions from their own, as something quite different from themselves. Each religion, it does not matter which, tries to dominate the other, and from that domination arises the spirit of aggressive proselytism, which is an immense barrier to Inter-nationalism. The priests of each religion, who should be the teachers and leaders of the people, want to work only for themselves, they want what we all want : comfort, pleasure, and all the amenities of life. Religion is no more real to them than to the rest of the people. A degraded priesthood is the curse of every religion, and yet we all encourage its existence by our acquiescence. Unfortunately, modern religion deals chiefly with the trivialities of cere-monial, and the times and seasons when it should be performed, rather than with trying to develop the right attitude towards our neighbour, whether he be brown or white, Brāhmaṇa or Pariah, aristocrat or plebeian. Hinḍūism teaches the Brāhmaṇa the way to Nirvāṇa, to attain Mokṣha, but it does not teach him—except in theory, to be forgotten in practice —that God is equally present in the Pariah as in the Brāhmaṇa, and that therefore he should show the outcaste the same reverence as he would show to God.

Mr. Lloyd George probably goes to church when he thinks fit, when he is not playing golf on Sunday morning, and imagines that he is a very devout Christian, pious, and all that is respectable. If I told him that he was not a Christian, he would be extreme-ly offended, and yet he acts in a most unchristian manner in politics. "Love your neighbour as your-self," says Christ, and Mr. Lloyd George will accept that statement in his private house, and for his own

Nation. But "love your neighbour Nation as you love your own Nation," he will consider as betrayal, as disloyal to his own Nation and to his own country. This shows us that religion accepts a double standard of morality, one for the individual as part of a particular Nation, and the other for the individual as part of the world. Religion teaches that to shoot your neighbour is wrong; that is, if he is your blood-brother or fellow-countryman. Legally such a crime is counted as murder, and punished by hanging. But to shoot your neighbour of a different colour, of a different nationality, of a different flag, is an act which not only religion but the whole world praises, and such action is decorated and rewarded with the blessings of the church. This attitude naturally creates a God with a National Flag. The idea of various Gods, sitting in various departments of life, each ruling a different Nation and waving a different flag, makes us smile. But ridiculous as it may appear when baldly stated, the result of so-called patriotism works out in that most absurd manner.

The League of Nations, which is now sitting at Geneva, instead of being dominated by ethics and religion, is dominated by fear, greed, and the principle of grabbing. Some little time ago I attended a meeting of the League at Geneva, and wrote down my impressions as follows:

I would not have it understood that I am against the existing League of Nations, indeed, far from it. It is one of the unexpected and beneficent results of the war; but only let us not blind ourselves to the imperfections of the League, for then only can we help to perfect it. One of the great disadvantages of the present League is that it is not a League of *all* Nations, and that an authoritative spiritual force is sadly lacking. I am not one of those who would cut down a fruit tree because it does not grow fast enough and give forth fruit, but I desire only to examine the tree to ascertain if it is really a fruit tree. I am convinced of the capabilities of the League, but they are too limited. Not one of us would be silly enough to deny the potentialities of the League, and it would be equally absurd to say that the League of Nations now sitting at Geneva is perfect, and that it can function with united and international will. As far as I could judge and from what I could gather from some of the delegates, each representative is mainly concerned with the interests of his own country. So that the true spirit of Internationalism is yet to be evolved. Indeed we should be more surprised, if it already existed. I am quite certain that the majority of the League would scoff at the idea that religion and politics must go hand in hand, if the latter is to be a spiritual force in the world. For them, as for the majority of politicians of to-day, politics must needs be kept in a water-tight compartment, lest such a vague unreality as religion should corrupt them, and if perchance the politicians happen to be religious, they would no doubt be afraid that the purity of their religion should be polluted by politics. They all, or at least some of them, go to church every Sunday, to offer up prayers to their particular deity, who, after Sunday, retires, to reappear again only the following Sunday. So this game of hide and seek with God is played in all departments of life, and particularly so in politics. I think it was Gladstone who affirmed that the two great interests of mankind were politics and religion; and one can unhesitatingly declare that so long as these two great forces are kept asunder we shall have neither a lasting peace nor a contented conscience. With this union must go the realisation of the oneness of *all* religions, for then we shall escape the many abominations that are committed in the name of religion, and the inhuman exploitation of a younger race for the benefit of so-called civilisation, which has been the characteristic of modern politics. The realisation that *all* human beings are children of God will alone give us the right to be arbiters of our fates, and to be the builders of a greater and a happier civilisation.

Now let us take the third subject—Business. I am afraid I do not know much about it, but I should like to suggest a few ideas that have occurred to me. Experts, naturally, are needed to handle such technical questions as tariffs, banking and exchange, international coinage, and a common script and language for the world. Some of you in the audience have studied these problems, and could illuminate them from a Theosophical point of view. The whole world is trying to tackle these problems to-day, but the experts look at them from an irreligious point of view, and therefore do not touch the foundation. We, Theosophists, believe in a religious foundation for life in its entirety, we must solve these intricate and delicate problems through our Theosophy. We must have our ideas and conceptions for the solution of all these problems. We cannot leave them aside for others to work out who are not religious. We must try to establish an International Board, to control the commerce of the world, not for the profit of a chosen few, but for the entire world. A curious thing is happening now in the West. The Allies are drawing near to their former enemies the Germans, whom they so much hated and abused; great German financiers are coming over to what was known as the enemy country, England, to arrange credits and organise trusts on an international scale, but unfortunately this Internationalism is at present strictly for the benefit of a few very rich people. Thus, international action is being forced upon us, though it is carried out in the wrong spirit, and for an immoral purpose, *i.e.*, to exploit the poor, the needy, the suffering, and this method, if it continues, will inevitably lead us to another war. We, Theosophists, have a special rôle to play in preventing these things. We must understand the problem, and must have our technical experts who will explain to us what is wrong, and then we must create, through magazines, through lectures, through propaganda of every description, a public opinion which is Theosophical.

Now let us take the fourth subject, which is rather a tender subject—Patriotism. Hindūism has taught us the doctrine of reincarnation, but Theosophy alone explains truly and clearly what is meant by reincarnation. We Hindūs are still content to believe that we are an especially honoured race, who reach Mokṣha naturally, and who are always reincarnated in this country, in India. We also have, curiously, the belief that Brāhmaṇas will always be Brāhmaṇas, and still more curiously, if we are men now, that we shall always be men, and never women. That is why we treat our women-folk in such a shameful and disgraceful way. If we really believed and practised this theory of reincarnation, our ladies would not always occupy the background as they do at present, and only appear when they are wanted. We are narrow, because we do not put our principles into practice. Luckily Theosophy demolishes completely this absurd theory that we should always remain Brâhmaṇas, or Shūḍras, or Pariahs, because we happen to wear those particular bodies in this life. On the contrary, it teaches us very distinctly and clearly, that we shall be born in every country, and even sometimes as women. The purpose of reincarnation is to give experience to the soul, and for this purpose we must be born into different Nations, into different castes, and different sexes. How absurd then, judged from this standpoint, is the patriotic cry, " My country, right or wrong ! " In moments of crisis, patriotism always overrides our principles, puts our conscience to sleep, and makes us incapable of judging facts truly. We, Theosophists, who preach from the housetop the principle of Brotherhood, fail lamentably in upholding the main object of our Society. Even Theosophists in allied countries were not immune from the poisonous wave of hatred caused by the war. I see smiles of superiority from Indian members of the Society, because they did not hate the poor Germans, but, believe me, our turn has now come when we must show of what stuff

we are made. We see hatred raging against the
Englishman in India, just the same hatred as existed
in England against the Germans. It is our duty, if we
are real Theosophists and upholders of Brotherhood,
the duty of each one of us, to stem the surging tide
of unbrotherliness, not only within ourselves, which is
more difficult to do, but also in the outside world.

Now, friends, we have examined some of these
problems which stand in the way of the unity of all
Nations. I want you to understand what is meant by
true Internationalism. An Internationalist is he
who lives, not like an ordinary man, but like a
superman, knowing himself as a God and saluting
the God in all other men. That is true Internationalism. We must aim at finding the divinity in each
man, forgetting the trivialities and pettinesses that at
present hide the light and magnificence of the
supreme God in him. Treat each man as you would
treat the Buddha, or Shrī Kṛṣhṇa or Christ. Thus
only will you understand, and at last develop, the
true compassion that heals all wounds and kills the
evil both in yourself and others. Behave in your
daily life as if you were cherishing the world, and
look for the Godhead in the sinner as well as in the
saint. It is so easy—so frightfully easy—to be
brotherly with the saint, but it is more difficult to find
the beauty of divinity in the sinner. Let our
service, then, be first to the sinner, and lastly to the
saint, first to other Nations, then to our own. Thus
shall we become true Internationalists.

————

THEOSOPHY AND THE IDEALS OF
EDUCATION

I count myself fortunate in being the first speaker at a Convention series of lectures to have his lecture presided over by our new and honoured Vice-President. Many other lectures of similar series he will doubtless chair in the years to come, but I take a little satisfaction to myself that my own address is the first thus to be honoured.

In endeavouring to speak on Theosophy and the Ideals of Education, I am confronted with a subject of very great difficulty. I confess I admire and envy the ease with which my very distinguished predecessors have spoken on their respective subjects. But may I wonder whether, had they to speak on education, they could have spoken with equal ease ? For my own part, I think there is no more difficult problem than the problem of education, for, although it is true that ever since the world began education has been taking place, we do not seem at the present time very far advanced in the direction of having established, once and for all, fundamental educational principles. We do not seem to be very far advanced in arriving

at a truly satisfactory system of education based on a
true understanding of the objectives of life.   In fact,
while we may be speaking about education, we ourselves need education.   Life is education and education is life.   My brother, Mr. Krishnamurti, has been
characterising us—and himself as well, I admit, of
course—in terms which are certainly clear and em-
phatic, though hardly laudatory.   I think it was only
yesterday that he told us that we are more or less
fools.   Now for foolish people to endeavour to lay
down definite ideals and principles with regard to any
question whatsoever is, to say the least, somewhat
presumptuous, especially so in the matter of education.
So in this talk I propose simply to deal with a few
points worthy, I think, of note, omitting many others
of equal, or perhaps of even greater, importance.

Mr. Jinarājadāsa has very kindly dubbed me an
educational expert.   But the more I study, and
certainly the more I study western advance in education, the more I feel how much I have to learn from
many wonderful pioneers who are blazing the educational trail for us to follow.   However much we who
are Theosophists—at all events members of the Theosophical Society; it is not quite the same thing—
however much we who are members of the Theosophical Society feel that we ought to be able to
regard ourselves as in the forefront of evolution
in many departments of life—and indeed we ought to
be in the forefront—there are many workers outside

our movement who are where we ought to be, and this is specifically true so far as education is concerned. I had hoped, if circumstances had not intervened, to tour the world in order to study the advances made by experts in the educational field both in Europe and in the United States of America. I should have immensely profited. That is now impossible. But we must realise that whatever has been done in the Theosophical field—and there is no doubt that we have done much in the educational plot—others have done equally good work along other lines, while some have done better work, even along our own lines. Hence it behoves us to make a special effort from the standpoint of education. We must put educational reconstruction on sound lines in the forefront of our Theosophical programme.

Now my task is to try to put into juxtaposition Theosophical ideals and education. And in order to do so I should like just to touch on a few points with regard to the history of education, so far as we know it at the present time. I should like to lay down the proposition that, so far as ancient India is concerned, the educational ideals towards which we are to-day progressing were thoroughly realised, by the few if not by the many. If the world as a whole—the western world included—is to proceed along sound lines with regard to educational reconstruction, we must turn to the East for assistance in the solution of many of the problems which are confronting

F

pioneers at the present time. My first proposition is, therefore, the fact that in ancient India the true ideals of education were known. It would, of course, be the work of one well-versed in the ancient Scriptures, and historical records generally, to give to us a clear and succinct analysis, not merely of the principles as they were known in ancient India, but of their application in the then everyday life. Such a task were well worthy the attention of some Theosophist well versed in ancient Indian literature. No more notable contribution to the science of Education could be made than the unfolding of the ancient Indian system of education, illumined by the Theosophical attitude. I am well aware, of course, that books have been written on the system of Indian education obtaining in ancient India, but not from the Theosophical standpoint, not from the standpoint which would give us a far clearer insight into the methods and principles than is possible to be given by those who look at ancient India largely from the standpoint of the external, the outer.

In ancient India, then, we can see the principles in existence, though I am not able to say to what extent they are likely to have been practically at work. That is a matter for the historian to tell us, but undoubtedly so far as the Scriptures are concerned, the ancient Hindū Scriptures, they do contain, as I know from translations, an adequate statement of educational principles. Modification may no doubt be necessary to suit modern conditions. The modern practice must inevitably differ from the ancient. But I believe that the eternal principles of education were known in ancient India, and that it is the task of the modern world to rediscover them.

Turning now to the West, I am inclined to believe that these ancient ideals were reflected in the earlier period of Roman history. If we study the earlier period of Roman history from the standpoint of education, we shall see how the mother is supreme, and how the educational system is permeated by her influence, as never since has the influence of women been felt, so far as regards the training of youth. One cannot help feeling that in ancient Rome these ancient Indian ideals are somewhat reflected; and what is of special interest is that in those days there was more or less of what we are struggling to obtain at the present time, namely, the balance between the need for individual growth on the one side and the need for the fulfilment of citizenship on the other. This is, in fact, one of the great problems of modern education—to reconcile the demands of individual growth with duty to the State, to the Nation, to the Commonwealth. This is one of the great problems of modern times, and has largely arisen since the War. In ancient Rome that problem was partly solved, realised, and worked out in terms satisfactory alike to the individual as well as to the State; with the result that Rome became great, with the result that Rome was able to extend her Empire and become the "mistress of the world". There is a great field for educational inquiry so far as ancient Rome is concerned; but when we go a little further back and look at ancient Greece, we find the idea of citizenship dominating, the individual being entirely subordinate to the needs of the State. So far as I am aware—I speak subject to correction —there was little in ancient Greece to correspond to the *Roma Dea* period of ancient Rome. I do not know that this ideal was exhibited in ancient Greece specifically along the lines along which it was worked out in ancient Rome. At all events it is clear that if you take ancient Greece as a whole, citizenship is everything, the growth of the individual matters not at all, save as it contributes to the welfare of the State.

Let me pass on to a later period with regard to ancient education, so far as the West is concerned, the period of decadent Rome, when the ancient ideal was entirely lost, when the Empire was given over to luxury, was given over to selfishness, to a complete spirit of narrow individualism. When we look at education in those days, we see how the ancient ideals are lost, and a spirit of narrow self-seeking, pleasure-seeking, empties education of its life, makes it the slave of man's lower nature instead of the channel through which the Divine force may flow. Hence the inevitable downfall of Rome, succeeded by the Dark Ages.

Passing from the Dark Ages, we come to the period of the sixteenth and the seventeenth and the eighteenth centuries when education is dominantly individualis-tic, though faintly we may perceive the shadow of that ideal of balance, crudely exhibited in the Rousseau idea of contract between the individual and the State. Reading the educational works of the leading educationists of those days, we see that while it is true that the individual aspect of education dominates, the individual being educated largely for himself, for his own purpose, his own growth, at the same time there is the idea of relationship between him and the State. From the seventeenth century onwards, that idea is undergoing a process of development. But the individualistic spirit dominates right up to the beginning of the great World War. Patriotism was not ignored, but for the most part it had but a second place. The individual was primarily educated for the purpose of competition and not for the purpose of co-operation, for self-interest and not for self-sacri-fice. Exceptions to the prevalence of that rule no doubt existed. There was and is that magnificent Boy Scout movement, which Sir Robert Baden-Powell has developed into a World-Brotherhood of Youth. There are also other movements of similar type, so that we realise that side by side with the individualistic spirit, with the narrower patriotism, there has been evolving a larger patriotism. Self-interest has gradually been balanced by self-sacrifice. On the whole, however, up to the beginning of the World War we were still dominantly individualistic in our education, we were following the spirit of competition, of self-interest, not of service or self-sacrifice. When the War came, there naturally had to be a change in the angle of vision. Citizenship mattered to the exclusion of everything else, and it mattered, I think I am not exaggerating, to the exclusion even of individual conscience. The claims of the individual conscience were made to yield to the dictates of the collective conscience—rightly or wrongly, it is not my province here to argue. I remember when I was in England in the very early days of the War the abominable treatment accorded to those who were really conscientious objectors. We saw citizenship domineering and crushing even conscience. The urgent need of the Nation made everything else of subordinate importance. The conscience of the few had to give way to the conscience of the many. So, during the War, there was the swinging of the pendulum from extreme individualism to extreme citizenship. And since the War, the educational experts in the West are asking themselves a certain vital question. They are asking themselves what, in fact, are the ends of education. Some time ago a lecture was delivered by the Principal of an English Training College, in the course of which the lecturer asked: What are the ends of education? Is there anyone to tell us what those ends are? Is there anyone to tell us to what end and purpose we are educating the youth of the country ? What, in fact, does citizenship mean ? What is the goal of citizenship ? In fact, the lecturer wanted an answer to a question which has been answered in Theosophical literature—What is the Whence, the How and the Whither of man ? And she wanted the answer put in terms of children. What is the whence, the how, and the whither of the child ? How valuable a contribution to the science of education might be made by some competent Theosophist who would exhaustively discuss the question of the whence, the how and the whither of the child, trying to explain to us clearly whence the child has come, what, in fact, is the essential constitution of the child, not merely from the outer standpoint. What is the pathway of evolution, and what the nature of the goal the child is born into the world to achieve ?

In this lecture it is somewhat of my business to try briefly to suggest to those educationists in the West who want to know what the ends of education are, that Theosophy answers this question exhaustively. Not, perhaps, in specifically educational terms, but in terms which can be translated for use in the educational universe of discourse. The truths we know through our membership of the Theosophical Society, which are summed up in the word " Theosophy," are all the truths we need for a foundation for the educational reconstruction of the world. But for the advantage of teachers, for the advantage of children, for the advantage of the educational world generally, those truths must be stated in educational terms. We want those forms to be adopted with regard to the expression of Theosophical truths which will be easily understood by, and acceptable to, those who are accustomed to think along certain lines.

Let us look at education as it is. What is still its dominant note despite the influences of the War? An enlarged individualistic note, whether viewed from the standpoint of the individual himself, or from the larger standpoint of the Nation. Even religion is made a matter for patriotism. There are as many Gods as there are Nations—each one apparently antagonistic to all the rest—at least potentially. In time of war God is invoked by each Nation to fight for it against its antagonists. So we see that even the "things that are God's" are narrowed down to subserve comparatively individualistic ends. Much more then must the case be similar when we consider the curriculum. I think it was Mr. H. G. Wells who said that wars are made in class-rooms, at least if he did not say it, he might have said it, and there is much truth in the statement. Take history as history is written and taught. In every history book the writer's Nation is inevitably exalted at the expense of other Nations. Take, for example, England and France. England is right in England and France in France. England is always wrong in France, from the standpoint of the French history book, and *vice versa*. In a word, the spirit of narrowness and of self-interest is definitely fostered by the history books we study. This is particularly evident in the case of Indian history books. Further, what is it that matters from the standpoint of most history books? War matters. Royal alliances matter. The deaths and births of royal personages matter. Treaties matter. The study of the growth of a people's Soul is only just now beginning to be given prominence as of dominant importance—the wars, the royal alliances, the treaties, being partial manifestations of that growth. Take mathematics. Where in the average school in any country is its soul-value appreciated and expressed? I was reading only the other day a book called *Mysticism in Mathematics*. I think those who are teachers of mathematics might read that book, and try to study how to put soul into a subject of immense importance in the development of character. With the help of Theosophy I am gradually beginning to realise that there is a profound meaning in the study of mathematics from the standpoint of character. In every school so many young people find this subject dry because it is not taught properly; because its value is not realised, not even by the teacher, so that he cannot convey the soul-value of his subject to those whom he teaches. Indeed, every subject of the curriculum is of definite value in the building of character, in giving those supreme gifts of education to youth—character and courage. For myself, I always look upon every subject of the curriculum from its character and courage building value. I test every subject by those two tests—does it build character, does it build courage? Does it help to inculcate that character and courage supremely needed in after life, that we may overcome the obstacles and difficulties that come to us as we tread life's pathway? I suggest that we should look at the curriculum from this standpoint.

Now the question comes as to how we are to try, as far as we can, to improve the situation. In a word, we must strive to re-establish the ancient ideals of education. What are they? I will suggest to you a few, as I understand them; those which, in my judgment, are of vital moment at the present time.

Now the first of these great truths is that the child is an age-old soul, however much the body is obviously young, comparatively new. Some years ago in Benares that principle was carried to excess. Let me here interpolate a little story. I remember how a young boy—he is not a young boy now—was selling literature outside the gates of the Central Hindū College, and someone came, someone older in body but not older in soul, and said to this boy: "You are very young to do this work." The boy replied: "I am only young in body, Sir, but I am an age-old soul." Perfectly true, no doubt. That shows how when these young people

listen to the lectures of their elders, they are able to
turn our statement very much to their own advantage
and, of course, not necessarily to the satisfaction of
those who think that they are older souls as well as
older bodies. Be this as it may, the fact remains that
the child is an age-old soul. We no longer can say
that a child is a body and has a soul. We say he is
a soul and has, from the standpoint of Theosophy,
many bodies.

My second proposition is that he has travelled
through all the kingdoms of nature. That is, his
consciousness has been stage by stage through the
various kingdoms of nature. He has gone through
infinite experiences of the world as a school. His
consciousness has passed through all the elemental,
the mineral, the vegetable, the animal and the human
kingdoms of nature. Each stage involves an ex-
pansion of consciousness, an added power, a wider
outlook. In the mineral kingdom consciousness is
asleep. In the vegetable kingdom it dreams. In the
animal kingdom it is awake and feels. It knows.
In the human kingdom it is awake; it feels; it
knows; and it is learning to know that it knows.
Self-consciousness is dawning. This brings me to my
next proposition—that just as feeling is the gift from
God to the animal kingdom, so is mind God's gift to
humanity. And with the development of mind comes
the growth of consciousness—the capacity to distinguish between right and wrong, which is the main

work for you and me. So far as the feelings are
concerned, we have been developing them before.
We have had more time to develop them, although it
is true that with the accession of mind their development becomes more troublesome than before. Hence
the supreme work of education is to recognise that it
is the conscience of the child that is primarily to be
developed. All must be subordinate to that end.
The curriculum in all its details is, whether we realise
the fact or not, intended to develop conscience, to
make it grow, so that we may come to the time,
which perhaps few of us have so far reached, when
the capacity has developed instantly, unerringly,
without compromise to seize the right and to reject the
wrong.   That is the goal so far as conscience is
concerned; and, even when we are looking at the child
merely from the physical standpoint, let us realise that
within there is an age-old soul; let us look for that;
let us look through the body at the soul, and not allow
ourselves to be glamoured by the fact that the body
seems, so far as the age goes, to contradict the soul.
It is doubtless difficult to imagine that the soul is as
old as our own, while the body is young. It has not
been imagined for hundreds, perhaps for thousands,
of years. It is part of the new contribution of Theosophy, of the new ideal in education, to realise the age-
old soul in the young body, and to equip youth to be
able to distinguish between right and wrong, unerringly and instantly: and to choose the right without

compromise, unhesitatingly, is the supreme goal of all true educational systems.

A vital contribution of the Theosophist to education is, as we have been told in previous lectures, the assertion of the fundamental Divinity of man, and of the gradual deification of man as the process of evolution. This fact, I venture to think, is of vital importance in education. The child is not only an age-old soul, but he is also, in essence, Divine, and he has the three great gifts of Divinity, of God to man, and of God to His creation—essential omnipotence, essential omniscience, and the time to make the essential real. These may be only in the seed, not even in the bud. They may be scarcely unfolded, but all are there in process of unfoldment. Time is, perhaps, the only gift of which we have any real cognisance, and if we could realise how great this gift of God is we might waste less of it than so many of us do. All of us are more or less wasting time, and yet time is, perhaps, the most precious of all the gifts, without which the other two could not possibly be achieved. Look at the child as potentially omniscient, as potentially omnipotent. And to make the potential actual, we have given to us time, and through education we must give courage. Without courage, time is of little avail. Is it too much to say that the supreme duty of the educator is not merely to give knowledge, but even more to give courage—the most useful of all qualities? Hence let Theosophists

strive to abolish despair, to minimise discour-
agement. Failure, of course, we cannot abolish.
Failure is inevitable, as is also success. Disappointment
is inevitable. But there is time to set against both of
these, and there is omnipotence and omniscience to
assure us of final triumph. Fear must go too, and
with it that odious corporal punishment which no
Nation ought to allow, and which some Nations, I
think, have forbidden by law. I was in an Indian
State the other day where a teacher said : " How can
we control boys if we do not punish them with a
cane ? " I replied : " If you cannot control the boys
without hitting them, then I would deny your fitness
for the office of teacher. Take up any other work,
but do not prostitute the office of the teacher or
besmirch the distinction to which you are called."
And some who heard me thought I was mad. But
one must be regarded as mad from the average standpoint, if one is to be a pioneer. Let us banish fear
and despair. I want every child to feel that every
failure can be a stepping-stone to success. I want
him to be willing to begin again, for if he is willing
to begin again, eager to begin again, he is learning
the lesson of failure, the power of failure. Let us
spiritualise education, base it on great ideals, so that
however much those ideals may fail so far as practice
is concerned ; so that however much those ideals may
have forms inadequate to their grandeur, neverthe-
less, the forms may be moulded and re-moulded,

so that by degrees the actual conforms to its archetype.

What shall I say about the teachers ? I have only time to utter phrases. I cannot enter into details. What is a teacher ? He is nothing more nor less than an ambassador, an ambassador from the eternal soul to its temporary dwelling-place, the body. Madame Montessori has, I believe, realised this fundamental relationship between the teacher and the child. She says that the teacher watches. It is the work of the teacher to watch, not to control ; not to give instruction, but to educate, to watch, to draw out that which already is there ; not that which has previously been put in, but that which is already there waiting to be expanded. Such is the whole function of the teacher. He is the ambassador from the soul to the body ; that is, the interpreter of the soul's function. Herein lie the real difficulties of the teacher. How is he going to interpret ? How is he to discover what has to be interpreted ?

On that point I should like to suggest that we must push the relations between Theosophy and psychology further than they have so far been pushed. We have one or two books on Theosophy and psychology, but we need more books. Psychology has advanced tremendously during the last few years, and in psycho-analysis, for example, we have a by-path, certainly dangerous, but at the same time of great value if properly and discriminatingly used. Further, the great experimental work in psychology proper

being done by great educationists, is of profound
significance to the educationist, and I wish the
Theosophist could enter both these fields and work
from above, from the ideal, showing that each well-
verified exploration into consciousness is to be understood as giving us insight into God's Plan, working
slowly but surely towards its triumphant fulfilment.

We have in India, for example, the caste system,
four great divisions of human temperament and
activity. We also have the four āshramas, the four
periods of human life. The caste system, however
much degraded in practice at the present day,
fundamentally means four types of service to the
State, to one or another of which each individual
belongs. There is the service of the Brāhmaṇa—the
learned man, the purveyor of Wisdom to the Nation.
There is the service of the Kṣhaṭṭriya—the man of
valour and of courage, who protects the Nation.
There is the service of the Vaishya—the merchant;
he who accumulates wealth for the Nation and dis-
tributes it in the Nation's service. Then there is the
fourth division—a general division, the server who
cannot specifically be classed in either of the three
preceding types of service. How valuable the power
to discriminate at an early age the type to which the
child belongs! How much time saved; how much
efficiency gained for the Nation! How much
dissipation of energy saved if we could so analyse
character as to be able to judge in good time the

best line of development for a youth to take, that both social service and self-realisation may be harmoniously blended to their fullest power and value. I myself have endeavoured to experiment a little in this direction during my many years ot educational service in India, and I have come to the conclusion that this field of inquiry is well worth exploring, and the Theosophist is, on the whole, likely to achieve therein the best results. It is largely, at present, a matter of Theosophical psychology.

Then as to the āshramas. How much more disciplined and purposeful our lives would be were we to recognise that there are these four great divisions— the stage of the student, the stage of the householder, the stage of the councillor, the stage of the sannyāsi —he who has retired from worldly pursuits, worldly cares, and worldly affairs generally, who is preparing for the regeneration which is called death, but who lives as a saint, to be an example to those who yet live in the earlier stages. I believe that some Western writers are already dividing life into periods, and I was lately reading a book wherein were given five great stages from infancy to maturity. A study of the Eastern Scriptures would clarify much that in the West still remains tentative. And the Theosophist can do much in this direction. We Theosophists have access to truths of evolution of deeper significance than those known generally, and nowhere more than in Education is needed a broad knowledge

G

of God's Plan of Evolution, as well as how to determine roughly the place and line of growth within that
evolution occupied by those whom it is our business
to serve through education. Looking at any individual child, the questions inevitably arise : Whence
comes he ? What is his pathway ? What is his goal ?
The more unerringly we can answer these questions,
the more truly can we educate. It is fundamentally
our business to help the child to do better that which
he has to do, in fact, not that which we think he
ought to do, still less that which we should like him
to do.

What is the note of all growth, from the standpoint of Theosophical ideals ? From a certain standpoint and up to a certain period of growth, it is self-
seeking, *i.e.*, self-assertion, but from the standpoint
of the future, from the standpoint of the majority of
the human race to-day, it is, as our President has so
often told us, self-sacrifice. In some of the ancient
Indian Scriptures, where the principles of education
are set forth, the first principle of all true principles for
education is stated to be service. It comes first, and
the first work of a school or a college, of the teacher,
is to inspire the child, however young he may be,
with the spirit of service. Study is the handmaiden
of service, the means to achieve wiser service.
What is the value of history, of geography, of all the
subjects of the curriculum ? Their value is in giving us
a greater capacity to be of use to our surroundings ;

and in that service, in that use alone, is true happiness to be found. We must strive so to vitalise our educational system that through education in college and in school the pupil finds service and self-sacrifice desirable, and of all other pursuits the most worth while. The first work of the parent is to instil the spirit of service into the child, not merely to provide him with food and clothing, not merely to give him the love that satisfies the child, but rather to give him the desire to be helpful, first, in the home. So is it the duty of the teacher, corresponding to the parent in the wider home which is the school, to give the child the opportunity to express the spirit of service in the larger surroundings of school and college. How is this to be done, to be practically worked out ? I tell you quite frankly, I do not know. How are we to recast our education in terms of service rather than in terms of self-seeking ? How are we to breathe into every corner of our educational field a spirit of self-sacrifice which shall in no way conflict with our equally important *dharma* of self-realisation ? Indeed, it is the problem of education to-day to reconcile and harmonise self-realisation and social service, so that each finds its truest expression with the help of the other. How are history, geography, science, mathematics, and all the other subjects of the curriculum—how are they all to be taught, so to be expressed, that each is to be a straight road both to self-realisation and to self-sacrifice—showing that in self-realisation there is the truest sacrifice, and in self-sacrifice the truest realisation of the self? History to-day is mostly prone to develop self-seeking, self-pride, contempt for other Nations, a narrow sense of superiority, rather than that spirit of brotherhood and of strenuous effort, undeterred by failure, by misfortune, by defeat. I think Mr. H. G. Wells has pointed out that we need new histories—histories tracing the sure, though slow, growth of brotherhood, histories that shall develop internationalism and inter-racial comradeship. Would that such were available to the youth of to-day! It is the same with all subjects, of course, as I have already suggested. We may have grown by our antagonisms, our self-seek-ings, our pride, our efforts at self-aggrandisement, but we can only achieve through co-operation, under-standing and mutual respect—to which end the young world has just displaced the old.

Let us not forget, on the other hand, the place of self-expression and even of self-assertion in the growth of youth. We cannot do without them. We must realise that self-sacrifice cannot be the only force at work at our stage of evolution. We must allow the child his normal growth, his self-expression at first through self-assertion. Self-expression, self-assertion, self-sacrifice, self-surrender, self-realisation: these are perhaps the stages of growth for which we have to look. How are we to give the soul the opportunities to grow? I think that question is being answered, on the whole, better by the outsider than by the Theosophist. Freedom is necessary for growth, and respectful understanding on the part of the elder. This is what we have to give. And the freedom must be ordered freedom, constructive freedom, freedom that does not mar the freedom of others, freedom that does not satisfy the lower nature at the expense of the higher. Our greatest teacher, my elder brother, Mr. Leadbeater, has often had, while educating his pupils, to stand for the needs of the soul at the expense of the desires of the body, and has then, as a true ambassador from the soul, ministered to the real needs of the soul. I know how sometimes the body inevitably thinks the teacher unkind. But it is better to suffer this injustice than to be untrue to the service of the soul, to which the teacher is pledged. The soul longs to gain control over its new vehicle, and to pander to the body at the soul's expense is almost an act of treachery. If sometimes the child judges the teacher harshly, let the teacher be patient and firm in his sense of right-doing. Time will justify him, and the soul is grateful.

Just one word more. I want to lay stress on the words : " Heaven lies about us in our infancy," sometimes quoted by teachers, but rarely understood. Heaven truly lies about us in our infancy, because we have come thence—a fact of supreme importance for the teacher to know, for the events in the soul's life immediately preceding incarnation, are of pregnant significance in the influence they ought to exert on life in the outer world. Our difficulty is to keep heaven about us in our maturity, however much it may have been about us in our infancy. The child comes from the heaven world. That is a fact the Theosophist emphasises. He knows how the soul has been in the heaven world, how it has been planning and realising that which down here can at present be but dream and ambition. The heaven world is the realisation of the future, of the real, of the perfect, in the midst of the present, the fleeting, the imperfect; and gives us the desire to incarnate again for further struggle. Children sometimes have remembrance of that heaven world, a world for which, perhaps, they long in this outer world where all seems cold and hard. And the work of the Theosophist is to try so to make a heaven of this outer world, that he may keep the child in touch with the real heaven, although his feet may be placed upon the earth.

Surely, friends, there is no object of study or of service more alive with possibilities, more fruitful in its resulting benefit to mankind, than the study of he age-old soul learning to adapt its new vehicles to its own eternal purpose. The soul is the objective of the teacher's ministration—the bodies are but the means to the soul's end—and to the understanding of the soul, Theosophy offers truths of profound importance. I do not say that in Hindûism, in Buddhism, in Zoroastrianism, in Christianity, in

Islām, these truths are not present. But Theosophy gives special prominence to these truths; first, because they are vital to the world's growth at its present stage of evolution, second, because they are in danger—we live so much in time and so little in eternity—of becoming obscured, perhaps even forgotten. These truths are, as we all know, the truths of Brotherhood—a realisation of the potentiality of which is, I venture to think, now dawning upon the world; of Karma, the law of Justice; of Reincarnation, the law of Periodicity, of rebirth in form and in time, that the true meaning of the formless and of eternity may at last be realised. Study these truths, understand them in their application to life, and we come gradually to appreciate the nature of soul, and of the individual souls with whom, as teachers, we have to do. The method of learning cannot be set forth in a single lecture, nor yet in many lectures. Those who are ready to understand will learn, and I pray that the teachers of the world's youth are of the company of those who are ready to penetrate into the mysteries of the soul, and to give to the souls who are entrusted with the making of the world's immediate future all facilities for understanding the nature of that future and for moulding their vehicles to the appointed end.

I have left out much I should like to have included—there is so much to be said: there are so many ways in which these great truths can be put into practice. I have said enough to suggest to you that the study of the relations between Theosophical ideals and education will repay any attempt you care to spend upon it; and if there are some of us who believe in the Coming of the World-Teacher, who believe that there is a reconstruction process in course of development, let us realise the responsibility we have of showing to the young the nature of the pathway they have to tread. Our work lies in trying, so far as we can, to anticipate the future, to intuit it, to discern it, to imagine it, and then to bring it into the schools and colleges, as well as into the homes. So doing, we shall be able to give the atmosphere of the future to souls far more concerned with the future and with the world's future greatness than they are concerned with the present. They must know of the past. They must be trained to understand the present. But their eyes must be upon the future to which they belong and for which they are to be responsible to God and to their Higher Selves.